Dear Reader:

The book you are about to read is the latest bestseller from the St. Martin's True Crime Library, the imprint the *New York Times* calls "the leader in true crime!" Each month, we offer you a fascinating account of the latest, most sensational crime that has captured the national attention. St. Martin's is the publisher of perennial bestselling true crime author Jack Olsen, whose SALT OF THE EARTH is the true story of one woman's triumph over life-shattering violence; Joseph Wambaugh called it "powerful and absorbing." Fannie Weinstein and Melinda Wilson tell the story of a beautiful honors student who was lured into the dark world of sex for hire in THE COED CALL GIRL MURDER. St. Martin's is also proud to publish two-time Edgar Award-winning author Carlton Stowers, whose TO THE LAST BREATH recounts a two-year-old girl's mysterious death, and the dogged investigation that led loved ones to the most unlikely murderer: her own father. In the book you now hold, THE DARTMOUTH MURDERS, Eric Francis confronts a tragic double-murder case that electrified the entire New England region.

St. Martin's True Crime Library gives you the stories *behind* the headlines. Our authors take you right to the scene of the crime and into the minds of the most notorious murderers to show you what really makes them tick. St. Martin's True Crime Library paperbacks are better than the most terrifying thriller, because it's all true! The next time you want a crackling good read, make sure it's got the St. Martin's True Crime Library logo on the spine—you'll be up all night!

Charles E. Spicer, Jr.
Executive Editor, St. Martin's True Crime Library

Roxana knew she was expected at around 6:30 P.M., but when she pushed open the Zantops' front door she knew instantly that something was odd, something was wrong.

Instead of walking in to the aroma of one of Susanne's famous gourmet dinners and a warm welcome from a couple she had known for a decade, Roxana was instead met with an eerie silence.

"Susanne, I am here! Where are you?" Roxana called out. No one replied.

The house, as always, was neat as a pin. Stepping in on the gray quarrystone floor of the entrance foyer, Roxana paused and hung her coat in the closet to her right.

She called out again. Still nothing.

Trepidantly, she turned to check the small study that served as the Zantops' home office, at the very front of the house.

There, in an instant, she spotted her friends lying on the floor of the study. In her heart she knew that they were both dead.

The Zantops lay just a few feet apart, surrounded by separate pools of blood. The once-orderly study now looked like a hurricane had hit it.

Her heart racing, Roxana took one look at the horrific scene. Then she turned, grabbed her coat and her keys, and ran for her car.

She knew that the next house was just a hundred and fifty yards away through the trees. Quickly driving there, she skipped the doorbell and instead pounded for help on the wooden front door, full force. . . .

THE
DARTMOUTH
MURDERS

ERIC FRANCIS

St. Martin's Paperbacks

THE DARTMOUTH MURDERS

Copyright © 2002 by Eric Francis.

Cover photographs © Robert Perron.

ISBN: 0-312-98231-3

Printed in the United States of America

St. Martin's Paperbacks edition / April 2002

10 9 8 7 6 5 4 3 2 1

INTRODUCTION

The material in this book is drawn from well over a hundred interviews conducted by the author, some quite lengthy over coffee or dinner; others as short as one question back and forth in a hallway before colleagues could spot someone talking to a reporter.

Information was also drawn from a number of published and broadcast reports on this story that first appeared in *The Dartmouth, The Dartmouth Review, The Boston Globe,* the *Boston Herald, The New York Times,* the Associated Press, the *Rutland Herald,* the *Times Argus,* the *Valley News,* the Manchester *Union Leader, People* magazine, *The Early Show,* and WMUR-TV Manchester, WNDS-TV Derry, WCAX-TV Burlington, WHDH-TV Boston, and New England Cable News.

There is still much more to be known about the Zantop case. The investigators have turned over the information gathered from their massive efforts to both the prosecution and the defense teams but the first the public or the press will likely see most of it will be when the trial commences sometime towards the spring of 2002.

It is important to remember that the courts and the juries in the United States of America have always, and hopefully will always, put the burden of proving the guilt of any defendant firmly upon the prosecution, in this case the State of New Hampshire, by presuming that the defendants are innocent unless proven otherwise beyond a reasonable doubt.

The jury is still out; thus, this book is not a legal judgment about whether or not Robert Tulloch and James Parker were actually responsible for the homicides of Half and Susanne Zantop. That question is reserved entirely for the judicial system to answer in a set of fair trials under the close scrutiny of both the public and a free press. This book is about the murders of the Zantops, the circumstances surrounding their deaths, and the apparent reasons that a nationwide, multi-agency task force that looked across the country and around the world for suspects felt confident that they had found them in a small town in Vermont—reasons with which a grand jury agreed with the authorities to the extent that it found probable cause to return two separate first-degree murder indictments.

ACKNOWLEDGMENTS

There are many people who helped during the course of this investigation that I would like to thank.

Foremost among them is my mother, ace reporter Janet Francis, who worked alongside me through so much of this effort. She tracked down leads day and night in all kinds of weather and became a walking reference of times, places, and people that was invaluable in writing this book.

I'd also like to thank fellow reporters Abigail Nitka, Rick Friedman, John Dillon, Doug Belkin, Franci Richardson, Harry Weber, and Victoria Block for their insights as the case unfolded and for their friendship during the many weeks we all spent in Hanover and Chelsea attempting to unravel this mystery for our respective readers.

From the literary world I would like to thank Jane Dystel, Maria Eftimiades, Fannie Weinstein, Charlie Spicer, Anderson Bailey, Henry Kaufman, and Alan Berolzheimer for their encouragement and assistance.

I would especially like to thank those whose insights put specific elements of the senseless events of January 27 into clearer focus for me. Among them are Katherine Almy, Susan Almy, Assistant Attorney General Kelly Ayotte, Richard Birnie, Andrew Crow, Nancy Crumbine, Mike Dunbar, Bruce Duncan, Kevin Ellis, Police Chief Nick Giaccone, Alexis Jetter, Audrey and Bob McCollum, John O'Brien, Carol Olsen, Annelise Orleck, Bob Sherman, Leala Tomlinson, and Brooke Wetzel.

Finally, in the midst of the shock and sadness that swept Dartmouth College this year, members of the Dartmouth Public Affairs staff swung into action to assist the dozens of reporters that arrived to cover the case. They helped defuse the understandable tension that arises when a community that has been deeply scared and hurt suddenly finds itself asked to share its closest thoughts with strangers. In particular I would like to express my gratitude to Roland Adams, Sue Knapp, Laurel Stavis, Tammy Steinert, and Dartmouth President James Wright.

prologue

The frenzy had come and gone. The shouts, the struggle, the screams, the racing of the attackers' car fleeing back down the driveway . . . all had faded.

Hidden just off the small main road leading down into the tiny village of Etna, New Hampshire, the snow-covered house and the surrounding forests which swept downhill towards the distant mountains remained completely silent as the chilled January afternoon wore on into the early evening.

At first the home's interior was lit by the abundant daylight that reflected off the white snow blanketing the adjacent meadow. But as the pale winter sun sank and the shadows of the tall surrounding trees crept gradually over the property, the lights throughout the first floor, and especially those inside the small study at the front of the house, became more prominent.

A brief snow squall had passed through mid-morning. In the afternoon the sun had briefly returned and the air had warmed slightly, but as evening approached, the temperature outside was plummeting back down and an icy breeze was starting to blow through the pines, birches, and maples.

On the oak floor of the study two bodies lay still, face down, surrounded by pools of blood that, as they continued to cool, went from a bright cherry red to a deep brick color.

Nothing moved, nothing stirred as the sun sank deep into the woods to the west and then slid behind Balch Hill, already obscured on the horizon by the dense trees.

chapter 1

Compared to Etna, Hanover is the big city. Compared to a real big city, Hanover may as well be Etna.

Separated from each other by the woods covering the Balch Hill ridge line, the two areas have had their own distinct character for the past two hundred and forty years. Hanover, New Hampshire, is a bustling college town. Etna, New Hampshire, is a quiet rural neighborhood, one of those tiny, tiny New England places that even people who have lived in the region their entire lives would have a hard time giving directions to.

The village of Etna and the area surrounding it that goes by the same name have been a part of the town of Hanover since before the American Revolution. Etna managed to hold onto its own small police, fire, and public works departments until 1963 when the village precinct was officially abolished and its miniature municipal government was quietly folded into the greater town of Hanover's.

The rolling green meadows and towering forested ridges surrounding Etna used to be home to dozens of small hill farms. In a little valley where the Mink Brook ran strong three months out of each year, a half-dozen seasonal water-powered saw mills and grist mills were once clustered along with a shingle mill, a cider mill, a wool-carding mill, and a cloth-dressing mill, all under the shadow of Etna's plain white Baptist church.

Today Etna village is still just a couple of dozen antique clapboard-and-brick houses surrounded by picket fences and bunches of wildflowers dotted on either side of the Mink Brook where the mills once stood. Interspersed among the homes are a small general store that still sells local maple syrup and grain along with national newspapers and coffee; a post office with 475 boxes that's been tucked inside the old school house; a one-room brick library which the locals lovingly built in 1906 on a foundation of solid granite before trimming it out with an intricately lapped varnished hazel wood ceiling; and a volunteer fire-department sub-station with a couple of fire engines and a tanker.

It's something of a New England tradition to have two distinct explanations as to how everything got its name. Usually the more straightforward, boring explanation is the correct one, and the more fanciful, elegant explanation is the cover story developed by descendants filling out their D.A.R. membership forms.

Etna was originally named Mill Village, but there was another hamlet with the same name within the community of Goshen, New Hampshire, and by the 1880s it became clear that neither place was ever going to get all its mail on the first try unless one of them relented and thought up a new name.

Depending on who you believe, the name Etna was either picked one morning in October, 1884, when Town Clerk George Bridgeman got sick of sorting the misdirected mail and, looking around his office for a suitable name, spotted the Aetna Insurance Company calendar and figured the name would be easier to spell if the silent "A" was dropped; or it was picked following a town-wide contest from an entry by two local ladies who had seen the word in a crossword puzzle clue that referred to Mount Etna in Sicily.

Again, depending on who you believe, Hanover was either named for the parish in Connecticut where the town's original colonists were living in 1761 when they got the royal charter allowing them to move north, or it was named for the House of Hannover in honor of King George III of England, who had granted the charter.

Either way, since 1769 Hanover has had one reason to be: Dartmouth College.

When the Reverend Eleazar Wheelock packed up his Indian Charity School and moved it from Connecticut to Hanover, he sent one of his prize pupils, a Mohegan Indian named Samson Occom, back over to England for a year to raise money for Wheelock's new college.

Occom, by then a preacher in his own right, impressed Wheelock's patrons, who sent more money over to help educate other Indian youth in the New World. It was a charming vision and the new college in the deep north woods, named for Lord Dartmouth (who wrote the largest check), certainly excelled as an educational institution— although only a handful of Native Americans graduated during the first couple of centuries, an irony that the college has worked hard to correct in recent years.

These days the Connecticut River serves as the state line dividing New Hampshire from Vermont, but back in 1778 Hanover and several neighboring towns seceded from New Hampshire. They joined forces with a like-minded group of Vermont towns and tried to form the state of "New Connecticut" with present-day Hanover to be designated the capital under the new name of "Dresden."

When plans for New Connecticut fell through, Hanover kept its name and, along with the other renegade New Hampshire towns, it instead joined the independent Republic of Vermont. That alliance also faltered, and Hanover rejoined New Hampshire in 1784 and started sending representatives to the new state legislature in Concord (Vermont joined the United States as the fourteenth state a few years later in 1791).

Today Hanover has a population of 10,000 people, over half of whom are Dartmouth students and graduate students. Most of the rest either work for the college or are closely tied to it.

Sitting on a hill a quarter mile in from the edge of the western boundary of the state, where the Ledyard Bridge links New Hampshire with Vermont, the Hanover Green is both the center and the heart of the Dartmouth College campus, and the focal point of Hanover's small downtown.

Main Street in Hanover holds the college's bookstore, the town's movie theater, a number of upscale restaurants and cafés, and, of course, the Gap store that no Ivy League campus could long survive without. The town's commercial district and the campus go hand-in-glove together, and then quickly fade to houses that run for about a mile in all directions before the woods loom back up.

While Dartmouth has long since evolved from the drafty wooden halls where Daniel Webster once read leather-bound books by candlelight, into the billion-dollar, park-your-corporate-jet and name-your-new-building, globe-spanning high-tech Ivy League extravaganza that it is today, Etna, by contrast, has continued to drift along through a kind of rural time warp that saw few changes until farming began to diminish in the late twentieth century, and brush and trees began to grow taller in what had once been neatly cleared fields.

In the past twenty years Etna has shifted from being a self-contained community in its own right, to becoming a bedroom community for the college and the massive Dartmouth–Hitchcock Medical Center. With the average cost of homes edging nearer to half a million dollars apiece, the tenor of the residents has gone from mostly country dwellers to mostly upscale intellectuals posing as country dwellers.

Crime is nearly non-existent across the entire town of Hanover. Dealing with alcohol, and some drugs, accounts for at least a third of the incidents in the police department's case log.

During the entire twentieth century, Hanover had just three homicide cases and, surprisingly, all four victims were students at Dartmouth.

In 1920, Dartmouth junior Henry Maroney was hunted down and shot dead in his room at the Theta Delta Chi frat house by a bootlegger named Robert Meads. Meads told police that he had sold Maroney a quart of liquor earlier that evening, but that Maroney later returned and demanded another bottle. Maroney wanted the additional liquor, but he didn't have another twenty dollars to pay Meads for it, so he simply grabbed it and ran. Infuriated, Meads tried to shoot Maroney on three separate occasions over the course of the evening, before finally tracking him to his frat house bedroom and succeeding. Despite the seemingly pre-meditated nature of the evening's events, the jury only convicted Meads of manslaughter and sentenced him to twenty years at hard labor.

In 1949 a stupid argument involving a bunch of Dartmouth football players, all veterans of World War II, who had been out on the town drinking, crossed the line into homicide when eight varsity players broke in and began ransacking the study of underclassman Raymond Cirrotta. When Cirrotta, who played on the freshman football squad and who had served with the Army in Tokyo, was discovered in his bedroom wearing a varsity sweater instead of one displaying just his class numbers this was considered such an affront to football etiquette and good-sportsmanship that Cirrotta was severely beaten. Varsity player Thomas Doxsee was accused of dealing out the fatal head injuries to which Cirrotta succumbed several hours later. Doxsee was fined $500 and received a suspended one year prison sentence after pleading no contest to manslaughter. After a sustained public outcry, and newspaper editorials that alleged an attempt was being made to sweep the whole matter under the carpet, a grand jury was convened to continue the investigation. A year later another varsity player, William Felton, was indicted and pled guilty to first degree manslaughter. Felton was fined $375 and given a suspended one year sentence and five years probation. All of the players involved in the fatal incident were eventually suspended by the college and were never re-admitted to Dartmouth.

There followed a forty-year lull in major crimes in Hanover until, out of the blue, a gruesome double beheading occurred in an apartment right in the middle of the downtown.

Shortly after the sun came up on the morning of June 17, 1991, a spurned Ethiopian graduate student who was playing hooky from a university in Sweden took out an ax that he had bought at Kmart two days before. Earlier in the week Haileselassie Nega Girmay had been turned down on his marriage proposal by Selamawith Tsehaye, and, seething with rage, he had hidden the ax in the apartment she shared with her friend Trhhas Berhe, a fellow Ethiopian graduate student. The two 24-year-old women had been sent by their families away from their war-torn homeland to study astrophysics in the safety that Hanover afforded.

Girmay threw away both of their promising lives, and his own, in a bloody 5 A.M. rampage. Neighbors heard the commotion and immediately called police, who arrived within moments. But the killings were over so fast that the first officers arrived just as the girls' screams subsided.

It was an open-and-shut first-degree murder case. Moments after the killing spree ended, Girmay, alone in the apartment, covered in blood, with the ax and the mutilated bodies in the room behind him, opened the door to the police officer pounding outside. Detectives didn't waste a lot of time wondering who-dun-it.

While at the time the deaths of the two shy, polite foreign graduate students certainly saddened the college and the town, the murders happened on Dartmouth's summer break, when the bulk of the students were away. Hanover was never in any doubt as to the suspect's identity or guilt and Girmay had no connection to the area other than his infatuation with a girl who had only been there a short time and who was barely known outside the Physics Department.

Girmay's lawyers tried for an insanity defense, but the New Hampshire jury looked at the cab ride to Kmart, five miles away in Lebanon, New Hampshire, and the two days the ax lay hidden. The jury quickly decided that, far from exploding in a jealous rage, Girmay had plotted his course of action for over forty-eight hours before striking when the victims were most vulnerable. Rejecting the notion that Girmay was anything other than a sane, stone-cold killer, the jury put him away for life without parole.

The Hanover police officer who knocked on the door of 8 Summer Street that bright June morning when Girmay answered was Patrick O'Neil. O'Neil figured he had seen Hanover's first and last double murder. Ten years later lightning struck twice, and O'Neil was supervising the night shift when the calls began coming in for the Zantop residence at 115 Trescott.

chapter 2

It had been dark for over an hour when the headlights of Roxana Verona's gray Saab snapped on and swept towards the beginning of Trescott Road.

To Verona, a full professor of French and Italian at Dartmouth College, the brief drive through Hanover that led to Trescott Road's undulating course was completely familiar. The college is bordered on the west by the Connecticut River which divides New Hampshire from Vermont, and on the east by the wooded ridge line whose summit is Balch Hill.

At first, so close to the college, there were houses lining the street on both sides, many with picket fences and painted wooden shutters. This late January evening, several houses still sported strands of Christmas lights running along the eves, or just the single plain candle in each window that is a long-standing holiday tradition in northern New England.

Quickly East Wheelock Street began its steep climb and within a minute's drive of the college, the houses began to thin, becoming farther apart and drifting farther back from the pavement as the woods took over.

Verona drove this route often on Saturday evenings. She was headed on a seven-minute trip to the home of two of her dearest friends: Half and Susanne Zantop, a high-powered husband-and-wife team of professors at Dartmouth.

A striking couple, the German-born Zantops were at the center of Dartmouth's social whirl. Tall, distinguished-looking, with a dry sense of humor and sporting a salt-and-pepper beard and mustache, Half Zantop, 63, was a professor of economic geology who had taught in Dartmouth's Earth Sciences Department for 25 years. Shorter, sprightly, and bursting with an irrepressible energy, Susanne Zantop, 55, had once been known more as a wife and mother at the college. Then she re-established her academic credentials by commuting to Harvard for her doctorate, and began a stellar trek up through the ranks. Susanne soon became a tenured Dartmouth professor in her own right, wrote several well-received scholarly books, and was eventually appointed the Chairwoman of the German Studies Department.

The Zantops traveled the world, frequenting Germany and Latin America, but when they were in town, they were in the habit of inviting Roxana Verona, a 54-year-old native of Bucharest, Romania, over for dinner, usually two, and sometimes even three, Saturdays each month. It was a ritual of friendship that had begun in the wake of Verona's husband's death three years earlier, when the Zantops were searching for a way to comfort the recent widow, and it had grown into a custom that all three took for granted as part of their lives.

As Verona's car rose farther and farther above downtown Hanover, the homes faded behind and her headlights began to trace out only the encroaching trees. Several feet of snow had drifted right up to the edges of the road, and soon along the way there were steady glimpses of low, hand-built stone walls, antique relics of the region's distant farming and sheep-herding past.

In the daylight there would have been brief but sweeping views through the trees of the mountains that rise on either side of the Upper Connecticut River Valley. On a clear day the view can stretch west across to central Vermont and the peaks of Mount Ascutney and Killington in the Green Mountain chain, while to the east, nearby Moose Mountain blocks off the view of the Presidential Range of the White Mountains that rise in central New Hampshire. But in the late January twilight, only the occasional yellow "WILDLIFE CROSSING" and orange "PUBLIC WATER SUPPLY—NO TRESPASSING" notices flashed out at Verona from amongst the towering Eastern white pines and stands of birches.

It's at the top of the road, or, as the locals call such places, "the height of the land," that East Wheelock Street officially ends, right where it is intersected by Grasse Road. From there on, as the pavement bends sharply to the right and begins descending down to the east towards the tiny hamlet of Etna, it becomes known as Trescott Road.

Less than half a mile above Etna's center, Verona passed straight through the T-intersection where, to her left, Woodcock Lane came in and joined Trescott. To her right, below her and beyond a patch of woods, was a flash of light from the Zantops' house. In a moment it was obscured again as a stone wall rose up along a small knoll on the right-hand side of the road and Trescott nosed even more abruptly downhill toward Etna.

Seconds after Verona passed the Woodcock Lane intersection she slowed and turned right, into the Zantops' driveway. Flanked by two short stone walls, the driveway entrance is hard to spot even in daylight. In fact, from Trescott Road it's nearly impossible to see the Zantops' house even though it is only a stone's throw away. The house sits behind forty yards of trees and brush at the base of a slope thirty feet below where Woodcock Lane runs into Trescott Road. If they are heading east, the most a passing driver ever sees of the residence is a fleeting glimpse of the standing-seam metal roof and the chimneys. If they are heading west and happen to glance down the curving driveway, they might notice a sliver of the south façade with a few windows, but in a second the brush would once again obscure the home, even in winter.

Viewed from Trescott Road, the entrance to the Zantops' driveway begins well to the left of the house. It then angles sharply back to the right along the base of the wooded slope, paralleling the roadway for about a hundred yards as it sweeps past the front of the house over to the attached garage on the far right-hand side.

By day the gray wood-sided contemporary house, with its slanted metal roof, sits above the lip of a broad meadow that rolls down to the south. Beyond that, on all sides, is the surrounding forest, part of which hides a stretch of the Appalachian Trail less than a mile away.

But at night the closest trees near the Trescott Road side of the residence dominate, and all is dark except for the lights of the house itself. It was those warm glowing lights throughout the main floor that now beckoned Roxana Verona.

Roxana stepped out of her car onto the inch of fresh snow that dusted the driveway. In the dark she didn't notice the faint red footprints ringed in blood droplets that led from the front door a few feet away.

Roxana had been here countless times before, and she had already spoken once this day to Susanne Zantop on the phone. At 10:30 A.M. the pair had confirmed their plans for dinner this evening.

Susanne and Half were always careful to keep their doors locked, but since it was just Roxana for the evening, and since Half was planning to put in a brief appearance at an elderly colleague's birthday party across town before returning for dinner, Susanne had made a special point of telling Roxana that on this night the door would be left unlocked and she should just come on in.

Roxana knew she was expected at around 6:30 P.M., but when she pushed open the Zantops' front door she knew instantly that something was odd, something was wrong.

Instead of walking in to the aroma of one of Susanne's famous gourmet dinners and a warm welcome from a couple she had known for a decade, Roxana was instead met with an eerie silence.

"Susanne, I am here! Where are you?" Roxana called out.

No one replied.

The house, as always, was neat as a pin. Stepping farther in on the gray quarrystone floor of the entrance foyer, Roxana paused and hung her coat in the closet to her right.

She called out again. Still nothing.

Puzzled, Roxana walked past the cherrywood Chippendale desk and its eighteenth-century banister-back armchair and towards the small hallway that ran across the far end of the foyer. To her right she could see lights on in the hall that led past the first-floor bathroom to the garage at the end of the house. Lights were also on in the hallway that led to the master bedroom and the stairway that rose up to the home's small second floor.

Listening harder, Verona couldn't hear anything towards the enclosed master bedroom, dressing room, and bath area. The utility rooms and garage beyond also seemed quiet.

Stepping through the archway to her left, Verona entered the main portion of the first floor—a large open area made up of the living room, the dining room, the kitchen, an enclosed greenhouse, and another enclosed porch at the rear of the house.

Richly paneled in natural wood with built-in bookshelves and cabinets, this section of the house had a Scandinavian-modern atmosphere accentuated by colorful wall hangings, antiques, and objets d'art the Zantops had collected during decades spent circling the globe.

Everything still appeared to be in order in the immaculate living room with its piano, leather sofa, Chippendale chair, and brass and Irish crystal lamps. Mexican silver bowls, silver candlesticks, and continental silver tea pots, tongs, spoons, and sugar bowls were untouched.

A two-foot-high Auguste Rodin sculpture of a nude female, entitled "Faunesse" and signed by Rodin himself—worth at least $15,000—stood in its place. Nearby, other shelves and walls showcased an even more valuable seventeenth-century painting by Dutch master Abraham van Beyeren along with other exquisite and expensive artworks,

etchings, statues, and antique books. All were undisturbed
in their accustomed spaces.

Expecting to see Susanne making dinner in the kitchen,
Roxana walked further into the living room and followed
the quarrystone path that wrapped around the large Nor-
wegian Jotul wood stove, just inside the archway before it
bent further to the right, skirting the oak-floored living
room and dining room as it wended its way into the kitchen.

The bright contemporary paintings and African textiles
on the walls of the dining room looked down on the empty
oval of the Danish Modern dinner table. In the spotless
contemporary kitchen, which was separated from the dining
room by a waist-high counter, some food was out, but nothing had been cooked.

Roxana called out again, trying to get a response from
her friends. Nothing. She had expected that Half might still
be out when she arrived, but she had every reason to believe that Susanne would be at home awaiting her.

Trepidantly, Verona turned to check the only other enclosed space on the first floor. The small study that served
as the Zantops' home office was an eleven-by-fourteen-foot
ell which jutted out from the living room at the very front
of the house.

There, in an instant, Verona spotted her friends lying on
the floor of the study. In her heart she knew that they were
both dead.

The Zantops lay just a few feet apart, surrounded by
separate pools of blood. The once-orderly study now looked
like a hurricane had hit it. A card table was upended, a
desk chair that had been smashed and splintered was lying
on its side. The rug was pushed up and there was a folding
chair that appeared to have been thrown. Blood was
splashed on curtains and on cabinets. A wastebasket had
been hurtled and papers from it had fluttered down everywhere across the chaos.

Susanne was lying just inside the doorway of the room,
face down, with a large pool of blood around her head.

Behind her was the overturned card table with one leg collapsed. Beyond the card table, Half was lying on his right side, facing into the room, with his head resting on the bottom shelf of a book case.

With the amount of blood and damage, it wasn't immediately apparent, but both of the Zantops had been stabbed at least a half-dozen times in the head, neck, and chest.

Half had what appeared to be defensive wounds on his left hand and left leg from trying to fight off an attacker before being disabled by a deep stab wound near the heart. The lower left pant leg of Half's blue jeans was soaked in blood, and more blood had pooled under his torso.

Susanne had put up a desperate defense herself, apparently wielding the folding chair as a shield. She sustained knife injuries to the right side of her head and neck before being taken down by a slicing wound to her abdomen. Chillingly, both the Zantops' throats had been slit, most likely from behind.

Sitting near Half's body, amidst the debris from the terrible struggle that had raged, was an Apple G4 computer with its monitor screen still glowing. It had been directed to the Web page of an Internet search engine designed to look up phone numbers and addresses, but no name had been entered. Nearby was a regional phone book with New Hampshire and Vermont listings that had been opened to the white pages under the letter "T."

Tracked across the scattered papers was a set of bloody boot prints that led from the middle of the murder scene, growing steadily fainter as they continued out through the living room, along the entrance foyer, and over the concrete front porch across a short section of snow-covered driveway, before disappearing where a car had apparently been parked. Another, less distinct series of shoe prints was also tracked across some of the papers.

Her heart pounding, Roxana Verona took one look at

the horrific scene. Then she turned, grabbed her coat and her keys, and ran for her car.

She knew that the next house, just a hundred and fifty yards away through the trees, was the home of Bob and Audrey McCollum and that Bob was a doctor.

Up to this point, Saturday, January 27, 2001, had been a good day for Dr. Robert McCollum. It was about to become the worst of nights.

The retired former dean of the Dartmouth Medical School, Bob McCollum had been celebrating his seventy-sixth birthday quietly with his family. They had spent the morning downhill-skiing at the nearby Dartmouth Skiway and returned in the early afternoon to spend the rest of the day in their contemporary beige-stuccoed cubist home, which Bob liked to joke seemed better suited to Southern California than to Northern New England.

Sitting just west of the Zantops' house, the sweeping view from the McCollum home's southern-facing windows looked down across the same common meadow to the dense woods beyond, but the two houses themselves were obscured from each other by a thick peninsula of trees and brush that jutted from Trescott Road down into the meadow.

Audrey McCollum, also 76, a retired Manhattan psychotherapist who had written several books about coping with trauma, and about her long-time friendship with a Papua New Guinean women's rights advocate, had made Bob's favorite birthday meal: a cheese fondue accompanied by Swiss wine. Their daughter Cindy and son-in-law John had traveled up from New York City to join them for the occasion.

The family was in the kitchen and had just finished the last round of dips in the fondue pot when Roxana Verona raced down their long driveway and pulled to a frantic stop underneath the well-lit front portico of the McCollums' house.

Roxana skipped the doorbell and instead pounded the wooden front door full force.

"It was a shocking interruption," recalled Audrey, the thought of the night's events still bringing tears to her eyes. "There was just an appalling banging at the front door. An obvious terrible urgency."

Cindy was seated closest to the door. She jumped up and ran to answer it.

On the porch, her car still idling behind her under the lights, Roxana was obviously distraught.

She began to pour out her story, her accented English fragmented to near incoherence by her panic. "I went to have supper," she sobbed over and over. "They said, 'The door will be open. Just come right in,' " she repeated.

At first the McCollums couldn't grasp the problem, but then Roxana started talking about calling out and nobody answering and not seeing the Zantops until suddenly she noticed they were lying on the floor. Instantly Bob McCollum's mind flashed to the quirky jury-rigged wood stove that the Zantops often used to heat their home. He thought it was possible that they had been felled by carbon monoxide poisoning. But then, in the flood of information she was trying to convey, Roxana got to the part about all the blood.

Cindy and Bob bolted for the door, Roxana close behind them. Audrey grabbed the phone on her kitchen wall and dialed 911.

"Cindy is not a doctor, but she works at Memorial Sloan–Kettering in New York and she's very attuned to medical emergencies," Audrey said. "They sped out of here. Cindy's car was positioned so she could get it out first and Roxana's car was still idling. Bob and Cindy went in Cindy's car. Roxana followed in her own car. I stayed to call 911. In a situation like that, our son-in-law John simply picked up *The New York Times*, which was an indicator he hadn't a clue what to do."

The first the state of New Hampshire learned about the Zantop double homicide was at 6:43 P.M., when Audrey's 911 call rang in at the Bureau of Emergency Communications in Concord.

"I was the first caller. I hadn't a clue," Audrey said. "All that I knew was that we had been told that two bodies were lying on the floor in a pool of blood."

Audrey was clearly worried, but she didn't know what had happened at the Zantops', just that two friends were down and they needed an ambulance.

Dispatchers in Concord classified Audrey's one-minute-and-thirteen-second call as a request for "medical assistance" and relayed the information back to the Hanover Emergency Dispatch Center in the combined fire station/police station building just a mile north of the Dartmouth College campus.

Twenty-eight seconds after Audrey McCollum hung up with Concord 911, a red-and-white Hanover Fire Department ambulance pulled out of the station with its lights flashing and began rolling towards Etna, two miles away.

Cindy, Bob, and Roxana burst back through the unlocked front door of the Zantops' residence and rushed towards the study. It took Dr. McCollum one look to determine that they were all too late.

"Bob realized they were beyond any medical assistance," Audrey said. "They had been dead a long time."

Cindy went into the Zantops' open-plan kitchen to grab their phone, but the portable handset wasn't in its cradle. After a few moments of frantically canvassing the area, Cindy found it and punched in the digits for 911. Her call reached dispatchers in Concord exactly one minute after her mother next door hung up with them.

Cindy told the dispatchers that the ambulance couldn't help, that her father was a doctor, and that he had just confirmed two people were dead. The Zantops were face down, and Bob, knowing he was standing in the middle of what would momentarily become a crime scene investigation, didn't want to turn them over, so it was difficult for him to be sure how they had been killed.

The 911 call from the Zantops' kitchen lasted just thirty-eight seconds, but it was enough time for the dispatchers to scare the willies out of Cindy. They asked her if there was a way she could get back out of the house in a hurry—because the murderer might still be lurking somewhere inside. "That hadn't entered our minds," Bob admitted.

Forty-five seconds after Cindy hung up with Concord, at 6:47 P.M., Hanover Emergency Dispatch radioed Hanover Patrolmen Brad Sargent and Steve Schlosser and asked them to respond to 115 Trescott Road. Sargent and Schlosser each switched on the blue lights above their respective cruisers and stepped on the gas.

Huddled inside the front door of the Zantop residence, experiencing a mixture of profound shock, sadness, and horror, Roxana Verona and Bob and Cindy McCollum waited anxiously for officials to arrive.

"It felt like an eternity waiting for the police, but I wasn't looking at my watch, so it could have just been five minutes or ten minutes. It seemed like forever," Bob recalled.

The Hanover police cruisers beat the ambulance to the scene and signed off in Etna at the Zantop residence in just under six minutes' time.

It was 6:53 P.M., and the night was just beginning.

chapter 3

The first cruiser to arrive at 115 Trescott was driven by Officer Brad Sargent. Sargent drove down the driveway and pulled to a halt behind Cindy McCollum's and Roxana Verona's cars. This brought to at least twenty the total number of individual tire impressions that had rolled up and down the length of the snow-dusted driveway since the killers had sped away.

Officer Steven Schlosser arrived at almost the same moment as Officer Sargent. He parked his cruiser on Trescott at the end of the driveway and ran down to the house.

Sargent and Schlosser entered the house a second apart, took one look at the carnage, and determined that they had a major crime scene. They moved to secure the area until their supervisor and detectives could be called in to take over the case.

While Schlosser looked around outside the front of the house, Sargent tried to comfort the three stunned friends as he worked the radio and the phone getting the pieces of the investigation into motion.

When they arrived on the scene, Patrick O'Neil and the other Hanover officers did a brief check of the Zantop house and grounds, looking for anyone else who might be hiding, injured, or dead. Satisfied that the main scene was confined to the study at the front of the first floor, they backed off and waited for detectives to arrive. They knew that what was needed now was a detailed "processing" of the scene by forensic criminologists.

Hanover police dispatchers began paging all the senior

officers in the department with the blunt message, "Two bodies on Trescott."

New Hampshire is small enough that every one of the state's murders is automatically investigated by the New Hampshire Attorney General's Office and the New Hampshire State Police's Major Crimes Unit. Hanover's nineteen-member police department is well respected within the region, but even when contrasted with largely crime-free neighboring towns like Lebanon, New Hampshire, and Hartford, Vermont, the town of Hanover has almost no experience with violent crime.

The Zantop murder was clearly going to be a large investigative effort, and the first thing the Hanover police needed to do was explain to the detectives and criminologists responding from across the Granite State where Etna even was.

Shortly, Hanover Police Chief Nick Giaccone arrived on the scene. As the evening progressed, five investigators from the New Hampshire State Police Major Crimes Unit would arrive, including the commander of the unit, Major Barry Hunter, and Trooper Jamie Steinmetz, who normally patrolled the region around Hanover, and who had now been deputized over to the MCU to help with the workload.

Waiting just inside the entrance of the Zantop house, Roxana Verona, Bob McCollum, and his daughter Cindy answered question after question for an hour as more and more detectives arrived and tried to make sense of the scene.

Meanwhile, next door, Audrey McCollum had no idea what was going on a hundred and fifty yards away through the woods. "I waited, and I waited, and I waited, and then I called Hanover Dispatch directly and said, 'Are your emergency people at 115 Trescott?' and the dispatcher said, 'Yes . . . They are,' and there was something about his tone of voice that let me know it was something very bad," Audrey recalled. "I was anxious, but I knew that it wouldn't be appropriate to go over there."

Searching for answers, and now growing concerned about Bob and Cindy as well, Audrey picked up the phone again and called the *Valley News*, the regional daily paper in neighboring Lebanon.

Audrey had written various travel articles for the publication over the years and knew Sunday editor Steve Gordon. She also knew the paper had radio scanners that monitored local police radio channels.

"Steve, something awful has happened next door; have you heard anything on the scanner?" she asked.

"No," Gordon said. "Oh, wait a minute."

After a pause, Gordon came back on and somberly explained, "They are saying, 'two down at 115 Trescott.'" Gordon told Audrey that in the context the police were using "down," it could well mean "dead."

An hour after they had first raced away, it was time for Bob and Cindy to make their way back home. Cindy and Roxana's cars had been ordered impounded where they had been parked so police could distinguish their tire tracks from any others in the driveway that might be of interest.

A police officer walked the pair back up Trescott Road and down their driveway. It was a cold winter night, and Bob and Cindy had turned their shoes over to detectives to be used to distinguish their footprints from others on the porch and in the house.

"In the rush of going over there we couldn't think about much because it was a matter of getting there," Bob McCollum said later. "But getting there was just devastating. You never anticipate anything like that, or how you will react. Then it was a matter of waiting for the police and having to sit there until they could release us."

"It was close to an hour when I looked out, and Bob and Cindy were walking up our driveway with a police officer with them, with a flashlight," Audrey remembered, beginning to cry. "By the way Bob and Cindy were moving, and the expressions on their faces, I knew it was terrible. I called out to them, 'Don't tell me they're dead,' and

Cindy said, 'Mom, come into the house,' and we did. It was unbearable.

"Bob has told me that with all the horrors he has seen as a physician, he has never seen anything that affected him so deeply," Audrey whispered. "It was so terrible."

"It wasn't just death. I've seen that," Bob said. "But these were friends in their home. It was sudden, senseless, and deliberate, and whatever you've seen, nothing prepares you for that."

Nothing had prepared the Dartmouth College campus either.

Although the murders were discovered only four miles from the Hanover Green, the center of Dartmouth College, news of the tragedy didn't begin reaching most of the 6,800 students and the faculty and staff until much later in the evening.

Dartmouth doesn't have a journalism school, but it does boast the nation's oldest college newspaper. Shortly before 9 P.M., someone monitoring a police scanner called in a tip to the news room of *The Dartmouth*. Normally on a Saturday night, the paper's offices, in an elegant brick building overlooking the Hanover Green, would have been deserted. By chance, *The Dartmouth*'s editor and president, Omer Ismail, 21, had stopped in, and he picked up the phone for what was to become the biggest story of his budding career.

Ismail quickly called two other college reporters to back him up. Reporter Mark Bubriski swung over to the paper with a friend of his who had a car, and picked up Ismail. The three headed for the address they had been given on East Wheelock Street. Back at the office, reporter Julia Levy had come in, and she began searching the phone book looking for the names of professors who lived on that street.

Not realizing that the scene was actually a few miles past where East Wheelock became Trescott, the three were confused by the lack of activity. They put a call through to the *Valley News* and found that they too were working the story. A sympathetic reporter gave the college students a better address, which they looked up on the Internet search engine Yahoo before they headed back up the road. This time they found the cluster of police cruisers parked along the stone wall in front of 115 Trescott.

When the guys called Levy back at their news room she was able to match the address to the Zantops'. Armed with the name, Levy put a call in to Dean Edward Berger, who confirmed that the couple were dead.

At 11 P.M., New Hampshire's state-wide television station, WMUR in Manchester, put out a report saying that there had been a murder in Hanover, but *The Dartmouth* was now way out ahead of the rest of the media on the story. Typing feverishly, Ismail, Levy, and Bubriski posted the information on the paper's Website at 11:15 P.M. Within minutes their server was close to crashing due to the intense interest, and Ismail made the decision to do the twenty-first-century equivalent of an Extra. "We were getting a lot of traffic on our Web site, so we emailed every student," explained Ismail.

"Two professors are confirmed dead," the email with Bubriski's by-line began,

> and police are investigating the possible double murder late this afternoon at 115 Trescott Road in Etna, just miles from the campus, according to Dean of the Faculty Ed Berger.
>
> Professors Suzanne [*sic*] and Half Zantop died sometime Saturday evening, but the police told The Dartmouth that they could not comment until after the state Attorney General Philip McLaughlin issued a press release. The Attorney General was scheduled to speak Saturday at approximately midnight.
>
> The Associated Press is reporting that the bodies were found at 6:30 P.M. Saturday night by police and guests of the Zantops.

However, the state police told neighbors that there was "nothing to worry about," according to a local resident who spoke with The Dartmouth.

Berger said that police were investigating and he could not confirm any more details of the professors' death.

"I've already been talking to a number of folks from counseling services to set up critical incident debriefing for students and faculty," Berger said.

Suzanne Zantop is chair of the department of German studies, and Half Zantop is a professor of earth sciences.

Professor Bruce Duncan, a german [*sic*] professor, said he knew Suzanne Zantop well and said her death is "just a total shock." He said that he did not know of any marital or domestic problems.

Page Chamberlain, a [*sic*] earth sciences professor, told The Dartmouth that he was waiting for a call from the chair of the department but declined to comment further.

Berger said he is meeting tomorrow with Dean of College James Larimore and College President James Wright.

The Dartmouth will continuously update this report as information becomes available.

The blanket email instantly reverberated around the campus and to the college's many far-flung travelers around the world.

It was a Saturday night at Dartmouth, and despite the college's genteel veneer, many of the students have always prided themselves more on the fact that the school was the inspiration for the movie *Animal House* than that tea is still served each afternoon in the wood-paneled, book-lined recesses of Sanborn Library. On a good Saturday evening, many of the fraternities and sororities can quickly achieve a level of alcohol-fueled debauchery that would make the average logging camp operator cringe.

At the Tabard fraternity, in a scene that was repeated around the campus, a visibly upset student stepped to the microphone in the middle of the frat's "Disco Inferno" party and read out the news of the Zantops' death. Several students left the party immediately.

Even saying that the news stunned the greater campus and community is something of an understatement. Dartmouth and the towns surrounding Hanover on both the New Hampshire and Vermont sides of the Connecticut River are some of the safest in the nation. This was the last place that expected to endure this type of tragedy, and these were the last people their friends would have expected to have been the victims of this kind of crime.

chapter 4

While most of Etna slept its usual Brigadoon-like sleep, activity continued unabated at 115 Trescott. Unmarked cruisers from the state police department and attorney general's office began piling up outside, along with the logo-emblazoned van carrying specialized equipment from the New Hampshire State Police's Major Crimes Unit.

At first police thought they might be looking at a murder–suicide, but as midnight approached and detectives got a better view from the doorway into the study, the gathered officers began leaning toward a murder investigation, and the decision was made to treat it as a double homicide.

As the forensic specialists began working their way inch by inch into the study, taking pictures, cataloging items, and bagging samples, troopers with clipboards logged people in and out of the house. Somewhere in the middle of the effort, the clock slid over the midnight hour and it became January 28 . . . Superbowl Sunday.

Eventually the photographs were finished, the positions of the bodies had been stared at closely by detective after detective, sketches and graphs had been made and outlines had been drawn. The Zantops were lifted one after another, and placed in body bags that were zippered shut on the spot.

Out front in the pitch-black pre-dawn darkness, a *Valley News* courier drove down normally deserted Trescott Road and, maneuvering past all the clustered vehicles, shoved the Sunday paper into the green plastic newspaper tube hanging below the black mailbox marked "115." The headline read, "2 Bodies Found in Hanover: Police Investigate Deaths of

Dartmouth Professors." A hearse that had been called in from the Rickert funeral home in neighboring Lebanon was pulling up to the scene.

With a state police cruiser acting as escort, the bodies were driven in the hearse to the chief state medical examiner's office in Concord, and logged into evidence before dawn. Later in the day, the autopsies would confirm that the manner of death in both cases was homicide due to multiple stabbing.

As the sun came up, reporters and photojournalists from across the state and New England began trickling in, and trying to peer over the stone wall and through the tangle of woods at the activity below.

From the outside, there was no hint of the bloodbath that had broken out within the house. Two sets of cross-country skis still sat with four poles in their rack just outside the door beside the garage. Both garage doors were down, and the Zantops' Subaru Legacy station wagon and Volkswagen Jetta were parked inside where they had been left. Four separate woodpiles ringed various points around the house and a small sailboat stood on a rack under a blue tarp beside the garage where the woods were closest to the house. An empty boat trailer was parked nearby.

It ended up taking detectives and forensic scientists the better part of four days to process the inside of the house, but on Sunday, officers could be seen videotaping Roxana Verona's gray Saab in the driveway out in front of the attached garage, and carefully photographing and videotaping the snow-covered woods and meadow surrounding the house.

Since the snow depth in the field and the woods had drifted to three feet in places, it was easy to see where there were and weren't footprints around the house. Shivering in the icy breeze blowing down Trescott, news photographers using telephoto lenses could see footprints coming from the edge of the driveway a short distance into the woods. But they could also tell that whoever had walked off the driveway had gone right back to it after a few feet.

It was impossible to see the back of the house from Trescott, but again, reporters could tell that the slick metal standing-seam roof had been sending snow cascading down in sheets all winter long and had formed a berm of snow several feet high around three sides of the house. Only in front, where the driveway and the doors to the house and the garage were, did it appear that the berm had been shoveled away. Even though there were doors on the back of the house, where there was a solarium and a separate screened-in porch, it appeared those entrances were effectively walled off by snow in the wintertime and that if anyone had approached the house from those directions, they would have left obvious tracks.

Mid-afternoon on Sunday, the waiting reporters watched as officers walked out of the house carrying a folding chair wrapped in protective paper and what appeared to be a computer, also swathed in white paper. At intervals, several smaller brown paper bags of evidence were also taken out and placed in waiting unmarked cars.

Through the course of the day, the forensic specialists would bag, tag, and remove all the paperwork, photographs, documents, books, correspondence, index cards, compact disks, briefcases, clipboards, calendars, and even the theater tickets that were present in the study. They removed the doorknob and the deadbolt assemblies from the front door and took the caller ID devices from around the house. They carefully wrapped the Apple G4 and the Apple PowerBook computers along with their monitors, mice, printers, and other computer paraphernalia and moved them outside to the cars. The Zantops' eyeglasses, cell phones, Rolodex, and keys lay scattered amongst the chaos; and these were photographed, bagged, and removed to be checked for fingerprints and other clues. Finally, detectives cut away the blood-spattered sections of the built-in bookcase where Half's head had been resting, and sent the boards along to the lab for analysis.

Taken in its entirety, the murder scene confronting detectives inside the house amounted to a real mystery; however, amidst all the chaos and confusion of the routine items that had been flung about the study, investigators found two critical pieces of evidence.

Lying amidst the shambles of the study were two twelve-inch-long plastic rectangles with the letters "SOG" embossed on the hard black material. They were sheaths for knives, and when state police detectives checked, they soon discovered that they were made for one type of knife and one type of knife only . . . the SOG Navy SEAL 2000 combat knife.

Although they were determined to keep the information from the growing legion of crime reporters forming up on Trescott Road, the detectives knew that they were now sitting on a clue that could potentially solve the entire case . . . if only they could trace the sheaths back to their owners.

The sheaths also told police something else that might not otherwise have been obvious. The fact that there were two sheaths most likely meant that there had been two knives wielded and therefore two killers.

The presence of the sheaths in the study also strongly suggested that the knives had initially been concealed, and hadn't appeared in the killers' hands until they got that far into the house. Otherwise, the tremendous struggle that the Zantops had put up in defense of their lives would more likely have started right inside the front entrance. Instead, it now appeared that one or both of the Zantops had answered the door and walked the killers into the study.

This suggested that at least one of the killers was someone the Zantops knew; although another possibility was that the killers had appeared innocuous enough and had a plausible enough pretext for being at the house that they were invited inside the study, even though the Zantops didn't know them.

Hand in hand with the primary question of who had killed the Zantops was the haunting question of why the professors had been killed. Like a crossword puzzle, where the exhaustion of the "Across" section leads the reader to spend more time on the "Down" words, police tried to work the Zantop case from both angles in the hopes of jogging loose a clue. If they could figure out the motive for the killings, they would be so much closer to finding their suspects.

Normally an undisturbed crime scene is a godsend to detectives. This wasn't a body found dumped in a swamp six months after the murderer had fled the area. This was an intact, isolated house where the bodies had been discovered probably less than six hours after the killings had occurred.

Still, the scene at the Zantop household that January evening raised as many questions as it answered. In many ways it looked more like an assassination than a robbery or burglary gone awry.

Break-ins in broad daylight are relatively rare, and for all its quiet tranquillity, there are many less-traveled roads than Trescott to choose from throughout the region. Small town residents in New England are infamous for their ability to notice even the slightest activity in their neighborhood, and anyone going in and out of the Zantops' driveway on a Saturday afternoon less than a half-mile from Etna's center could reasonably expect to chance an encounter with another driver who might make note of their presence (in fact, police would later learn that someone had apparently seen the killers' car). Furthermore, the trail of bloody footprints led right from the study back out to the porch just outside the front door. There, police found two particularly distinct bloody boot prints with two prominent blood droplets right beside them. Both appeared to be headed right for the driveway and, presumably, a waiting car.

If the motive had been robbery or burglary, there were plenty of things in the Zantops' house for the taking. Less sophisticated burglars could be expected to miss the significance of the Rodin or the valuable paintings and antique books, but the killers had also bypassed the abundant silver in the front room, dining room, and kitchen, and the diamond-encrusted pins, earrings, and other jewelry that Susanne kept in her bedroom. Not to mention the expensive Apple computers, stereo equipment, televisions, and appliances all around the house. Despite all of the potential loot, nothing seemed to be missing. Neither did there appear to be any attempt to locate or take the cash that was in the residence. Even taking into account panic on the part of the killers following their deadly battle with the Zantops, it still didn't feel much like a break-in or a robbery attempt.

But if it was a planned killing, it was a truly bizarre one.

First of all, what kind of criminal (let alone two or more), busy planning to kill someone in the year 2001 in the most gun-saturated society in the world, would bring two identical black-anodized combat knives to do the job? It looked more like some kind of a sick fashion statement than a professional hit.

And if there was a well-thought-out plan to use the knives, why wouldn't the killers have taken a few extra seconds to stop and recover the knife sheaths before they fled? Their failure to do so was an incredible gift to any investigation that would inevitably follow. It was so glaring an error for a planned killing, that it led investigators to seriously consider the possibility that whoever had stabbed the Zantops had, on the one hand, prepared for the possibility before coming to the house (by concealing the knives on their persons), but on the other hand, had not actually planned on killing them until something, perhaps an argument or an insult, blew the lid off the situation.

The police were wrestling with all these questions as more and more investigators arrived in Hanover that Sunday afternoon to start tracking down clues. Already a flood of phone tips was beginning to pour in to the Hanover police station. But outside, the press had little to go on and police were not about to admit how baffling the crime scene inside appeared.

chapter 5

One of the curses of journalism is that often, on breaking news stories especially, some small misimpression will slip into the early reporting and almost no amount of clarification after the fact can shake it loose from public perception. In the Zantop case, it was the notion that Half and Susanne were in the habit of throwing open their doors and welcoming complete strangers into their home with open arms, feeding and housing them in the process.

The fact was that the Zantops were known to be generous with their time and their house for friends and with some acquaintances such as students. But it was rare for friends, and almost unheard of for students, to drop over unannounced. In many respects, the Zantops were very traditional when it came to things like manners and invitations.

There were some occasions when they had invited people they barely knew to stay in their daughters' unused bedrooms upstairs. But these were visiting professors from foreign universities, graduate students with a reason to be at the campus, and friends of colleagues who were involved in projects in which the Zantops had an interest. How much of a risk was it, really, when all these people were coming to them through the auspices of some of the most exclusive colleges and universities on the planet?

The reality of the visitors who came to the Zantops' frequent dinner parties contrasted greatly with some of the initial press reports that described the couple's hospitality. Many readers were left with the impression that the Zantops were running a cross between a freelance youth hostel and missionary soup kitchen out of their living room. This perception was further bolstered by reports of Roxana Verona's initial statements that the Zantops had told her to come right on in because the front door would be unlocked.

In fact, the Zantops were in the habit of locking their doors at all times and keeping their burglar alarm system set. Friends would later describe leaving past dinner parties at the Zantops' house and hearing the deadbolt click shut behind them as they walked to their cars. It was precisely because it was so unusual for the Zantops to leave the door unlocked that Susanne had made a special mention of it during her telephone call with Roxana that morning.

After two harrowing nights with little sleep, Roxana reiterated just that point at 5 A.M. on the morning of Monday, January 29, when she faced the cameras and told CBS's *The Early Show* that even for her, one of the Zantops' closest friends, it was unprecedented for them to have left the door unlocked.

In fact it was so unprecedented that, in the early stages of the police investigation, it served to focus some of the suspicion onto Roxana.

Whoever finds a murder victim is automatically given serious consideration as a suspect until they are ruled out. There are many reasons that a killer might want or need to place themselves at the scene of the crime, and many cases have been cracked because of a hard look at the "finder." Roxana didn't help her status in this regard when she seemed to change small parts of her story in a series of interviews with the press during the first forty-eight hours of the case.

Anyone can forgive the variations as being the natural product of stress and fatigue in the midst of a truly horrible experience, and Verona was up against the added element of her Romanian accent, which became more pronounced when she got upset.

Roxana told *The Early Show* about Saturday's events, beginning with Susanne's phone call to her in the morning.

"We talked on Saturday morning around 10:30 A.M., and she decided for a quick, light dinner. This was our customary way of finishing the week for 6:30 P.M.," Roxana told the station.

"So around 6:35 P.M., I was there, and I just got into the house, and the lights were on all over the house, nothing special, when I drove in," Roxana remembered.

"I rang the door but the door was unlocked. Actually, well, this was the first thing that was really unusual. So I got in, and I went on the right of the house in the living room, and again everything was perfect as usual. They have a very beautiful house. I went there. I was saying, 'Susanne, I am here! Where are you?' and no one answered, and then I turned, and toward the left of the house, in the study, it was a nightmare," Roxana continued.

"This perfect picture turned into a nightmare and they were there on the floor and dead, and obviously they were dead. So then I just ran away with my coat and my car keys, and I went to my car and went to the neighbors. I knew those neighbors," she said.

"When you spoke to Susanne in the morning, was she at all concerned?" asked the anchor person. "No, absolutely not," Roxana replied. "She was very happy to see me. It was a difficult week finished, you know, we were making normal plans."

"I understand that this couple was very generous with their home?" the anchor continued, apparently referring to press accounts of the Zantops' throwing their house open to strangers.

"Very often, but not every week," Roxana responded. "She would have parties entertaining students for a dinner, or for a lunch or a special occasion, at the end of the term, for instance."

"Are you worried?" the anchor concluded.

"I confess I'm a little scared because this is a very quiet community, and we know life revolves around the computer," Roxana said (she may have meant to say "community," not "computer," but it was 5 A.M. after an upsetting night). And nothing . . . you know . . . like the students . . . it's a home, like a big home, and suddenly something happen in that home, so we are really very worried and we want a solution," Roxana said.

Roxana gave similar accounts to several local newspaper reporters and, in the absence of anyone else to focus on, inadvertently raised some red flags amongst the gathering storm of speculation.

The seeming "problems" with Roxana's version of events at the time were that in some of her brief interviews she said she had seen Susanne lying in a pool of blood and then fled. In other reports she said that she saw both Susanne and Half lying in the study, and that she knew both the Zantops were "obviously dead" the moment she saw them.

Nobody would wish to be alone in the middle of a murder scene in the middle of the woods on a dark night looking for a phone, so Roxana fleeing the house before she paused to call authorities made some sense to investigators. However, when Roxana got to the McCollums', she led them back to the house instead of calling police. Based on what she told Audrey McCollum, the first 911 call was dispatched as a medical emergency.

Doctors and ambulances can't do much for anyone who is "obviously dead," and police began to wonder why this wasn't apparent to a Dartmouth professor.

Introducing additional people and several more sets of tire tracks into a crime scene is the last thing that investigators want. But it would make sense for a killer trying to obscure their trail and create a logical reason for their presence at the scene.

Another thing that struck observers as odd about Verona's account of the evening was that she said that all the lights had been on throughout the house when she pulled up in the dark.

The Zantops were notably concerned about conservation. In the winter they heated with wood, and in the summertime, Susanne was even known to collect dead flies from around the house and take them down to her backyard pond to feed to the frogs so as not to "waste" them. These didn't sound like the kind of people who would have all the lights in their house blazing away during the daytime. And yet what little information had been discussed about the time of death seemed to indicate that they had been killed hours before the sun set at 4:54 P.M. that Saturday afternoon.

Who, then, had turned on all the lights? And why?

The suspicion that quietly focused on Roxana Verona in the first hours of the investigation was just a taste of what was to come in the days and weeks ahead. Dartmouth College would have to cope not only with the loss of two of their own, but also with the dark realization that what, only the day before, had been an idealistic academic community made up of trusted friends, colleagues, and students, was now also a large pool of suspects.

The McCollums inadvertently helped steer further suspicion towards the campus when they told reporters that the Zantops had recently been counseling a troubled student even though the McCollums had urged them not to continue.

Audrey, a retired psychotherapist, said that after Half had described the distressed male student to her, she had urged him to refer the boy to a professional, because she thought the student sounded paranoid and manic-depressive.

Although the McCollums had never met the student in question, they wondered, after the murders, if he might not have been responsible.

It was a well-intentioned lead that didn't seem to pan out—and it was just the first of many.

chapter 6

Investigators don't like to step up to podiums and announce that they are dealing with a "routine homicide." For obvious reasons, it strikes the listeners, not to mention the families, as extremely callous. But the truth is, most murders, whether or not they are ever successfully prosecuted, are so straightforward that they end up with only minimal coverage, buried somewhere in the middle of the Metro sections and Regional Briefs pages of the newspapers.

Average American teenagers may watch something like 33,000 homicides on television by the time they are sixteen, but for every plot twist on *Law & Order* and every surprise ending on *Poirot*, most murders narrow down to a handful of likely suspects within the first few hours. Most murder victims just don't have that many people in their lives who might have developed a genuine motive to kill them.

Although no one likes to say it, most murders fall into routine catagories.

There was nothing routine about the pool of suspects in the Zantop case. On the one hand, there weren't any suspects. On the other hand, there were literally hundreds.

In the hours after the Zantops were killed, none of their friends could think of one good plausible suspect who would have had a clear motive and opportunity to kill Half and Susanne. The Zantops were surrounded by dozens of people whom they considered close friends, their colleagues admired them to a point bordering on awe, they were both immensely popular with students.

Both of the Zantops had plenty of opinions on politics, social justice issues, and how the world should be run, but in that regard the two of them weren't any more controversial than any other opinionated scholar. They lived bright, busy lives and traveled the world on an insulated wave of good will and camaraderie that typified a kind of Ivy League ideal. Nothing they had done or said suggested an obvious reason why anyone would want to kill them.

Yet there they were, irrevocably dead, and someone had murdered them in broad daylight in their own home in one of the pleasantest, safest communities in North America. Dartmouth paused and took a deep breath, and then five thousand intellectuals began to wrack their brains for theories that would explain what had just happened.

Suddenly everything that had ever been said and done around the Zantops took on new and sinister connotations.

Some remembered an angry confrontation the day before the Zantops' deaths in the office of Dartmouth Professor Dick Birnie, where Half and a student had shouted at each other in Spanish. The student, an English and Spanish major, came forward and was questioned. He explained that he had been friends with Half Zantop since taking his Earth Science course, and the "heated" exchange had been an ironic twist of words said to each other in jest. Academic humor at its lightest and best.

Others remembered a suspicious-looking man wandering the dorms on the eastern edge of the campus on Saturday night looking for a phone and asking if anyone had heard sirens, or seen police, or knew anything about a murder. It turned out to be one of the *Dartmouth* reporters trying to find the story.

Police requested the records from all the area taxi companies and learned of another student who had taken a cab to Manchester Airport in the middle of the night following the murders, repeatedly urging the driver to hurry. He was cleared after questioning when police verified that he had been summoned home for a family emergency.

Another male student was questioned for four hours and

raised eyebrows when he told *The Dartmouth* that he felt
he had been tagged as a "prime suspect." He told the paper
that detectives had asked him and his friends whether he
practiced Santeria, a Caribbean-based religion that can include ritual sacrifice of animals. The student angrily de-
nounced the investigation and suggested that police were
lost and scrambling for any shred of a theory.

This didn't go over well with New Hampshire Attorney
General Philip McLaughlin, who had arrived to personally
conduct the next daily press briefing and reassure the community that the case was being taken seriously. McLaughlin
told reporters who packed the weight room at the Hanover
Police Station that there was "nothing overtly ritualistic
about the killing," but, he cautioned, that it was hard to
know just by looking at the aftermath of a murder what
another person's rituals might consist of.

One theory that made the rounds would have been dismissed outright if it hadn't been for the gravity of the situation. It postulated that Susanne had been killed because
of her recent appointment to the "powerful" academic tenure committee, which decides who is and who isn't worthy
to attain the rank of full professorship at the college. The
main problem with that line of reasoning was that Susanne
had just been appointed and she hadn't even met with the
committee yet, let alone alienated anyone to the point they
were willing to kill her and her husband.

Police followed up on this lead and dozens of others that
poured in, but their main focus stayed at 115 Trescott Road.
Despite all the theories whirling around at the campus four
miles away, there was one simple, crucial fact that police
kept a lid on for five days. The Zantops had not only been
stabbed to death, but they had been practically hacked apart
in a brutal hand-to-hand fight that had raged across their
study.

Police have a word for such murders: Overkill.

An "overkill" is a type of murder all unto itself. Drunks
fly off the handle and hit their wives or girlfriends with the

nearest object they can grab, often killing them before they know it. Drug dealers shoot rivals and debtors in back alleys and from cars. Once in a blue moon rival cousins trying to inherit family fortunes will slip arsenic into each other's gin and tonics. But few killings in modern times take the form of a repeated stabbing with an edged weapon.

A stabbing is a horrific act. It literally places the attacker less than arm's length from the victim. Blood flies everywhere. Lots and lots of it. More blood than any TV drama would be comfortable showing. A victim can be expected to resist, to struggle, and possibly even to overpower and harm the attacker. A would-be murderer dispassionately planning a killing isn't likely to opt for a stabbing. It's simply a bad strategy.

So who actually stabs someone to death?

The answer tends to be someone who is extremely angry, not just mad, but angry to the point where they've crossed over into a blind irrational rage of a kind not often seen even in fictional portrayals of murders.

More importantly, murderers who stab people to death are not just irrationally angry people. They are very angry *at the specific people that they stab.*

Agree or disagree with the jury verdict, but a major point in the O. J. Simpson investigation was that detectives suspected O. J. right off the bat because Nicole Simpson had died in an overkill stabbing. Investigators felt that he was about the only person who would have known her long enough and intimately enough to become that enraged at her.

Police looking over the scene at the Zantop house felt the same way.

"The crime scene investigation did not reveal any evidence that the Zantops' residence was broken into, thereby indicating that the Zantops were expecting the assailant(s), or at least were familiar with the assailant(s)," wrote Detective Robert Eastabrook in a search warrant application he filled out three days after the murders.

In addition to the theory that sheer anger had motivated the stabbings, detectives also held open the possibility that one or both of the Zantops had somehow triggered an extreme fear reflex in their assailants that had quickly translated into an overkilling rage.

Whatever the exact reasons, police felt they were looking for someone who knew the Zantops . . . someone who knew them and harbored a secret, seething hatred towards at least one of them.

To find that person, investigators set out into the community to try and develop what they called "a greater understanding of the circumstances surrounding the Zantops' deaths": their friends, their colleagues, their students, their careers, their travels, their relationship, their interests, their passions, their principles, their ideals . . . in short, their entire lives.

Somewhere in the Zantops' shared history, investigators were looking for the thread that would link them to their killers.

chapter 7

Half Zantop was born right at the beginning of World War II, on January 24, 1938, in Eckernforde, Germany, the fourth child of a printer and his wife. The Zantop family had been living in Spain in previous years and they returned there again soon after Half was born.

His mother died when he was young, and his father eventually remarried and had two more children.

Half grew up on a relative's farm, speaking as much Spanish as German. By the time he was ready to attend high school his father moved the family to Barcelona, where he had bought a box-manufacturing company.

In an interview with *The Boston Globe*, Half's older brother Wolf Zantop recalled that, as a young man, Half was a good athlete who made up for what he lacked in raw talent with perseverance. "He was a normal young man, not the fastest, not the smartest, but he would work harder," Wolf Zantop told the *Globe*.

Half went back to Germany during his college years and earned a degree in Geology from Freiburg University before coming to the United States. In 1961 Half received another Geology degree at Washington State University and in 1969 he earned his doctorate at the Stanford School of Earth Sciences in California.

At Stanford, Half met another young German student named Susanne Korsukewitz, and began a relationship that would span half his life.

Susanne Korsukewitz Zantop was born on August 12, 1945, in the small German town of Kissingen. The oldest of three children of a brick-factory manager, she quickly impressed the teachers in her small farming community with her ability to master her studies. She was a happy child in a middle-class home who loved reading books, playing classical music on the family piano, and badminton games with her younger brothers.

"She was always the best or the second-best in class, but mostly the best," remembered her brother, Dr. Thomas Korsukewitz, now a gastroenterologist in Germany, in an interview with *The Boston Globe*. He told the *Globe* that he had last spoken to Susanne on the phone just days before she was killed, as they planned an 85th birthday party for their father.

After high school, Susanne had gone to the Free University in Berlin, where she earned a degree in Political Science. From there she went to California to attend Stanford, and earned a master's degree in the field.

When Half left for South America on his first major job assignment, Susanne went with him, and in 1970 the pair were married in Argentina.

By now Half was specializing in "economic geology," the branch of that field which looks at ores and minerals that are worth something to the mining industry. This can include the obvious "treasure" metals such as gold and silver, but also more pedestrian industrial commodities such as copper, zinc, and tin. From 1969 to 1975 Half worked as a senior geologist across the world for several large corporations with mining interests, including Kennecott Copper and Bethlehem Steel.

Half and Susanne and their two young daughters, Veronika and Mariana, had been posted in locations across South America, Spain, and Africa for the mining industry, but Half was growing interested in switching from a corporate to an academic career. In 1975 he returned to Germany, where he spent a year as a research fellow in ore microscopy at the University of Heidelberg.

In those days colleges still required mandatory retirement of professors at age 65, and in 1976, Dr. Richard

Stoiber, Dartmouth's professor of economic geology, had to step aside.

When the Dartmouth Earth Sciences Department began advertising in trade magazines that Stoiber's position was available, Half replied and quickly went to the top of the pile of applicants.

"Economic geology was a very important part of Half's credentials when we recruited him to come here," explained Dr. Richard Birnie, currently the Chair of the Earth Sciences Department at Dartmouth, and a close friend of both Zantop and Stoiber.

"One of the things that Dick Stoiber had done was mining geology so, since this department had a tradition of economic geology, we were very anxious to hire somebody who had practical, commercial, real-life exposure to the mining industry," Birnie said. "We advertised in our journals and Half applied. It was definitely his idea to begin an academic career. Half had worked in industry for years. He did work in Argentina, but also in Spain, in mineral exploration, and he has since worked in Mexico and Guatemala. The focus of much of his field work has been in Latin and South America. He would have been in high demand in industry or in an academic department."

Late in the winter of 1976 Professor Richard Stoiber and fellow geology Professor Jim Reynolds and his wife Haidee drove from Dartmouth north through Vermont and across the Canadian border into Quebec to pick up Half and Susanne and their two young daughters at the Port of Montreal.

Ten days before, the Zantops had boarded a Polish cargo freighter in Hamburg with a total of 22 suitcases, boxes, and assorted duffel bags and sailed for North America.

The professors' cars were parked a considerable distance from the dock, and the cargo port didn't have red caps or baggage carts. So after customs inspectors had stamped all the Zantops' paperwork, the men began shuttling the mound of luggage forward and rebuilding the pile at ap-

proximately hundred-yard intervals, while Haidee Reynolds, Susanne Zantop, and the two tired but excited young
girls guarded both the pile that was growing and the pile
that was diminishing. All this took place in a light, cold
mid-afternoon drizzle under the gray Canadian skies, but
eventually the Zantops and their possessions arrived at the
vehicles and everyone piled in for the trip south to Dartmouth College. Dick Stoiber would later joke that the
whole process reminded him of the stations of the cross.

As the professors drove on into the early evening, the
drizzle switched to a stronger and stronger rain as the cars
pulled up at the small junior faculty house where Professor
Birnie was waiting to greet them in Hanover. Despite the
chilled air and the rain that was now an outright downpour,
Dr. Birnie had gone out on his small porch, fired up his
barbecue, and was grilling up hamburgers and hot dogs to
welcome the new arrivals.

"Stoiber went over to the Zantop girls with a big, juicy
burger on a paper plate and said, 'This my dears, is the
American dream,' " remembered Reynolds in a letter to *The
Dartmouth* after the Zantops' deaths.

During the quarter century he spent teaching at Dartmouth, Half would become most widely known in the Earth
Sciences field for his work on the geology of several
regions in Mexico that are rich in silver deposits. But
amongst his colleagues and his students he was known as
a tremendously observant field geologist who could add
new insights on almost any geographic region of the world
that was under discussion.

From time to time Half would also appear as a guest
professor at the University of Heidelberg in Germany, and
do consulting for corporate mining interests around the
world. But mostly he was in class or out across the hemi-
sphere with his students from Dartmouth.

Because of his association with Dick Stoiber, Half
would also dabble in volcanology, the study of volcanoes,
although he never wrote any academic papers on the sub-

ject. When he took students on annual trips to southern Mexico to study mines, he would also make it a point to take them on side trips to see the volcanoes in the region.

During his first years at Dartmouth, Half and his students spent much of their field time in Guatemala, El Salvador, and Nicaragua, because Dick Stoiber and Dick Birnie already had studies under way in those countries. As Half gradually took more and more control of the direction of the field program, it started to focus in on Mexico, and for the last fifteen years of his career that was where the Earth Sciences undergraduate majors would spent an entire term with Half during their junior year at Dartmouth.

As one of eleven professors in Dartmouth's Department of Earth Sciences, Half taught several advanced courses, but he also taught the Introduction to Earth Sciences course designed for undergraduates who just wanted to see what geology was all about. This exposed him to a much wider swath of the general student population at Dartmouth and made him much more well known amongst the undergrads than some of the other Geology professors who only dealt with more advanced specialties. Standing six feet tall and frequently dressed in corduroys and natty sweaters, with his neatly trimmed salt-and-pepper beard and mustache and slight German accent (which many a female student remarked on finding sexy), Half was a popular ambassador for the entire field of geology amongst students who were still exploring possible majors in the sciences.

Each November Half would take about twenty of the geology majors out on a ten-week "stretch" of field study. The group started in Chesapeake Bay and traveled on to the Big Horn Basin in Wyoming, and then the New World mining district in Montana before working down through Death Valley to the Grand Canyon and spending the final two weeks in Mexico.

As 1998 Earth Sciences graduate Melanie Kay recalled in a letter to *The Dartmouth* about the Mexican portion of her stretch with Professor Zantop "Half was routinely the

first one awake, the most eager to stay in the field until
sunset, and the last one awake at night. And, he never ate
lunch. My fellow students and I could barely keep up. In
the evenings, we would sometimes filter into Half's hotel
room for cocktails and discussion, sometimes academically
related but sometimes just for fun. Then, somehow, while
we were all groaning at the 6:30 wakeup, Half was already
downstairs completing his leisurely breakfast. On that trip,
Half took us up a 15,000 foot volcano and down 1000 foot
mine shafts. He taught us everything from the best places
to shop in Guadalajara to the inner workings of the earth.
And he did it all with class, kindness, and humor," Kay
recalled.

"One day, Half took us all to a day off at the beach. He
ordered us all 'Coco Locos,' a fruity punch in a coconut
that he insisted we try. Then, with all of his 20-year-old
students, he ran into the water and bobbed in the waves
with the rest of us. This was a man who seemed very content with his life's work."

Half could be quiet and reserved, even somewhat dry
and formal at times, but there was also a warm and kind
side to him that students appreciated. During his years at
Dartmouth, Half served as an advisor on an exceptional
number of graduate and undergraduate theses.

"A lot of our majors are here because of Half," Professor
Birnie said. "Half could explain things well but also he
would explain his thought process, so you knew how he
got there. To me, it's an unusual property of a person where
you not only know their conclusions, but you understand
as a part of a conversation why they came to those conclusions. That's why I learned so much from him. It's a very
unique property in a person, and Half had it. He was very
articulate and very open in that way."

Half published a number of papers and articles in geology journals over the years and in the weeks prior to his
death, he was in the process of finishing a revised edition
of his 1988 book *International Mineral Economics*.

While Susanne had started out in the Political Science arena she would spend the better part of a decade and a half as a wife and mother before coming into her own as a scholar and a professor who delved into German, Spanish, Comparative Literature, and Women's Studies.

"Susanne came to the area a few years before, when Half took a job in the Earth Sciences Department," recalled German Professor Bruce Duncan. "She already had an MA in Political Science, sort of from a previous life, and she hung around the German Department a little, and she even audited a couple of classes, and then she decided to go back to school."

In 1980, as Half settled into Dartmouth, Susanne began commuting nearly three hours away to Boston to the University of Massachusetts, where she earned her master's degree in Comparative Literature. Then it was on to Harvard, where she was awarded her doctorate in German and Spanish in 1984.

Afterwards she taught for a period at Santiago de Compostela in Spain, where her specialties included eighteenth- and nineteenth-century fiction and the history of ideas.

Susanne joined the Dartmouth faculty in 1982 in Comparative Literature in German and Spanish, and formally joined the German Department in 1984.

In the mid-1980s Dartmouth began a program of leaning, though not over backwards, toward the hiring of spouses of professors. Before this decision, hiring one spouse to teach just because the other was already a professor was considered tantamount to nepotism, but as that attitude began changing, the Zantops were in a position to benefit.

An article in *The Dartmouth Weekend Magazine* in January 1986 noted that Half and Susanne were among forty faculty couples at the college where one spouse was tenured and the other was not.

"When my husband came here in 1976, I went back to school," Susanne Zantop told the magazine before her rou-

tine third-year tenure review. "I commuted for four years
to the University of Massachusetts at Amherst and to Harvard. It was good luck and good timing that positions were
open here when I finished."

"I'm really glad the college is encouraging the spouse
policy," Susanne continued. "There are so many cases of
separation because of lack of jobs."

Susanne was granted full tenure as a professor of
German and Comparative Literature in 1984 and she would
go on to become the Parents' Distinguished Research Professor in the Humanities and a professor of Women's Studies. In 1996 she became the chair of the German Studies
Department, a post she would hold until her death.

"Susanne was a very engaged teacher, imaginative, and
very, very dedicated to students. She really was an important person to a lot of students," said Professor Duncan. "I
think she became increasingly important to women students
because she was somebody who was able to combine marriage and a career and did so very successfully. That was
one of the remarkable things about their marriage, how they
supported each other's careers just totally . . . they really
were a team," Duncan recalled, adding, "They did things
together all the time. They enjoyed an awful lot of things
together. He was always sort of a calm, genteel sort of
person; she tended to be a bit livelier and more given to
opinions. They weren't that far apart, but he always seemed
to be running at a slightly slower speed. Absolutely seam-
less cooperation between the two."

At Dartmouth, Susanne was one of those constantly active individuals whom even busy people wondered at in
amazement.

Despite her numerous responsibilities, her scholarship
into obscure German poets and literary movements, her
multiple professorships, her ongoing manuscripts and journal review projects, her commentaries on women's issues
for National Public Radio, and a host of other wide-flung
interests, Susanne seemed to be able to work around the

clock. At the same time she kept a spotlessly neat house, played her piano, gardened, hiked and skied cross-country, cooked gourmet meals, and participated in a crammed social calendar that would make many full-time New York club hoppers blanch.

Susanne typically rose at 5 A.M. and started work in her home office. Then, just as the rest of the campus was rising, she would settle in at her wood-paneled office in the German Department, on one of the upper floors of a beloved old white Colonial-style building overlooking the Green, called Dartmouth Hall.

"She was always very busy, but at the same time there were always students in her office and she worked a lot one on one with people," said Professor Duncan, who had once chaired the department himself. "Susanne was just enormously energetic, and had a wonderful sense of humor, very, very lively," Duncan said, adding, "She was a good tennis player, enjoyed sailing, and just did a lot of things."

During her years at Dartmouth, Susanne wrote and edited eight books on German topics ranging from visual arts to women writers, but her best known work, in 1997, came from her unique study of the literature that accompanied Germany's late entry into the age of colonization. While England, France, and even Belgium were busy carving up large slices of the world, Germany was largely out of the Great Game. But that didn't prevent German travel writers from spinning fantastic tales that imagined Germans dealing with "natives," ranging from the women of the remote Brazilian jungles to American Indians.

In writing about, as she coyly put it, "Cannibals, Amazons, and Headless Men," Susanne had hit on something other scholars had missed, namely, how German travel writings, especially those about Latin America, had imagined a German colonial period that really didn't exist, but the longing for which set the stage for the World Wars of the twentieth century.

Susanne also picked up on the subtle and not-so-subtle

sexual overtones of much of the writings which imagined (largely male) German colonizers living in domestic bliss with the (largely female) colonized. She had hit upon the notion that, long before Germany actually set out to colonize parts of Africa, Latin America, and the Pacific, there was already a mentality, a collective desire for colonies, that had bordered on obsession within the collective German consciousness.

"Susanne was a really famous scholar. She was doing work that was recognized all over," said Professor Duncan. "One of her interests was post-colonialism, looking at the intersection of politics and cultures in dealing with Third World countries and colonialism. She was able to write without as much jargon as some, and write things that were more accessible to people who didn't already agree with that point of view. Her most famous book was translated into German by a German publisher, and that's kind of high praise."

That 1997 book, *Colonial Fantasies: Conquest, Family, and Nation in Precolonial Germany, 1770–1870*, was republished in 1999 by a German publishing house for the German market as *Kolonialphantasien im vorkolonialen Deutschland (1770–1870)*.

As individuals and as a couple, the Zantops were at the pinnacle of their careers. Each had earned a prominent role in their fields at one of the nation's top schools. In their quarter century spent together in Hanover, their academic contributions and insights had won them geniune high praise, not just within Dartmouth College's own ivy-covered walls, but from researchers and scholars around the world.

Among those who knew them, they were cared about deeply as collegues, as teachers, and above all as friends. They loved and admired their native Germany, and had lived in many other countries over the years, but along the way the Zantops had, almost inadvertently, lived out the first-generation American immigrant success story.

Arriving on freighters as foreigners and students, Half and Susanne had worked their way up through American society to become not only valued members of a single institution, but indeed to become respected members of the intelligentsia of their adopted nation. As 2001 dawned and the twenty-first century took shape, it was clear that the Zantops had every expectation, and every right, to look forward to continuing success in both their personal and academic lives for many years to come. Yet for all their accomplishments and acheivements, it appeared to police that someone, somewhere, had wanted them dead.

chapter 8

Both as private citizens and as Dartmouth professors the Zantops had traveled extensively around the world, and had friends and associates all over the planet. It soon became clear that police were also going to have to consider international suspects when it came to understanding the circumstances surrounding their deaths.

"The Zantops were members of not only the Hanover community but the national community, as well as the world community," noted the Senior Assistant New Hampshire Attorney General in charge of Homicide, Kelly Ayotte, at one of her early press conferences.

As Adjunct Professor Alexis Jetter, who teaches Journalism and Women's Studies at Dartmouth, put it, "They were people who were infinitely curious about the world. They spoke several languages. They traveled widely. They were hikers, and skiers and gardeners. They did everything beautifully," Jetter said. "They were European, they were very proper, but also very irreverent, a lot of fun. They were physically very beautiful people, but they were extremely modest and unselfconscious. They made their home a center of laughter and conversation and politics. They were very interested in justice.

"They were just people of the world in every respect. He took groups of students to Mexico City every year to study volcanology. They traveled all over the world, they knew people all over the world, and they brought people into their home from all over the world; but in recent years they became American citizens, because they felt they owed it to America to help set it straight," Jetter said with a laugh.

The Zantops maintained an apartment in Berlin that Susanne's parents had passed on to them, and both Half and Susanne traveled there frequently to do research and to lead Dartmouth's foreign studies programs in Germany.

They were in Germany when the Berlin Wall fell in 1989, and they quickly called close friend Eric Manheimer, the medical director of Bellevue Hospital in New York, and told him to drop what he was doing, pack his bags, and bring his wife Diana Taylor to join them in watching history. In 2001 it would be Manheimer's sad duty to act as the executor of the Zantops' estate.

On their own time, the Zantops led several tours and cruises for Dartmouth staff and alumni to places like the fjords of Norway and the glacial coasts of Alaska.

They had traveled extensively through Latin America and had once paddled together up a Guatemalan river in a dugout canoe.

In addition to traveling the world, the Zantops were fascinated by national and international politics, and liked to delve into what they and their friends called "social justice" issues. Together they stayed on top of world news as much as possible, and friends commented that they almost always heard National Public Radio on through the house when they visited.

"The word for them would be *gentle*," said English professor Dr. William Cook. "They were involved in most progressive issues that you can think of, from same-sex civil unions to Bosnia–Herzegovina."

"Susanne was very involved with women's studies, social issues, helping other young women on the campus. She was always commenting on NPR (National Public Radio) about women's issues. She was very feminist, very aware of women around here. She was a big example for me," Roxana Verona told the *Boston Herald*.

Susanne was a letter writer for the Hanover chapter of

Amnesty International, a humanitarian group that she had once worked for as a researcher in Spain. In January 1986 Susanne told *The Dartmouth* about a success that her group had had with a Moroccan student who was sentenced to ten years in prison because of his membership in a radical student organization.

"We corresponded with the student for three or four years," Susanne told *The Dartmouth*. "We sent him textbooks because he was studying engineering, and because of our protest, he was given more freedom within the prison."

"Both Half and Susanne were a very broad couple and had many conversations about world politics and presidential politics and all these kinds of things," noted Professor Dick Birnie. "It sounds trite, but he was definitely for justice and fairness. He would never let expediency come in the way of fairness and justice.

"I would say Half was the calmer, Susanne was the more high-strung. Susanne the more exuberant, Half the more reserved. They were different in that way, but it was a nice complement to each other," Birnie added.

Friends put much stock in the couple's German heritage for their profound interest in fairness and equality.

"They both grew up in Europe," Audrey McCollum noted. "Susanne primarily in Germany. Half partly in Germany and in Spain. It was a period of time in which Germany had imposed a blackout on teaching about the Nazi regime until Susanne was thirteen and policy changed. She told me one day vividly about the shock, the horror, the shame, the guilt that she and her classmates experienced when, at the first time, at thirteen, they became aware what their country had done."

Professor Alexis Jetter remembered the same aspect of their character. "They were both deeply moved by being Germans whose parents were of Holocaust age; they felt a deep sense of—not personal guilt, because that's not how they operated—but they were motivated in some part by what they understood about what happens when good people stay silent and countries can do terrible, evil things. They were motivated by what they knew of evil in the human soul to do good, and they were profoundly good people. They were inspiring people, they were fun people, and they were beautiful people," Jetter said.

"I really am quite convinced that is what aroused very early in her life her conviction that if people don't pay attention to what is going on in their country, that terrible things can happen," added Audrey McCollum.

"They were frequently firing off emails to the Congress or the Senate. Once they reached a conviction, they would do everything in their power to inform themselves and become active. They were both catalysts in activating other people to notice the world they live in and to find out what the critical issues are," Audrey said.

History Professor Annelise Orleck noted that as a student, Susanne had worked in Spain organizing Spanish housewives who opposed the repressive nationalist government led by General Franco, and she had lived there after Franco's regime fell. Orleck said Susanne had taken away a deep insight into the need to preserve individual rights from that experience.

"When they decided to become US citizens three years ago, it was difficult for them to give up the country they had grown up in and had relatives in still," Orleck said, adding that when the Zantops decided to become Americans, "They made a profound commitment to this country and to trying to continually heighten awareness and encourage people to act. It's for this reason that I think their loss is an international loss," Orleck said.

Professor Bruce Duncan said he thought over and over again about whether their international involvement had made the Zantops any enemies. "They had firm political beliefs, but they tended to correspond amongst liberal faculty, so they weren't controversial in that way. She had only come on this CAP committee [the committee which recommends faculty promotions] this year, and she hadn't done anything yet. I can't imagine anything that would have caused anybody in any rational way to have been in conflict with her.

"What people are saying about them is true," Duncan said. "You want to speak well of the dead, but you don't have to put any effort into it with them. You couldn't help but like them. They had strong convictions, but they were tolerant. They really were remarkable people who just meant an awful lot to everybody in one way or another. This is really unimaginable. There's really no explanation I can think of except a random crazy act."

Both the Zantops (and their daughters) were fluent in English, German, and Spanish, and traveled widely and frequently. Audrey McCollum related how she and Bob and the Zantops would mainly communicate back and forth by email rather than pick up the phone or walk over their common back meadow, and frequently they'd be surprised by how far the Zantops had ranged in a day's time. "Often I'd send out an email with a bit of news, or a greeting, and the response would come from Berlin," Audrey said. "They would go to Berlin for two days and come back. She and Half were also involved in translation of one of their books into German, so they were coming and going at a speed that sometimes staggered us."

One of those staggering emails came on Sunday, January 28, less than a day after their bodies were discovered. To make room for Saturday's birthday celebrations, the McCollums had disconnected their computer. When they plugged it back in on Sunday afternoon, they discovered an email had been sent to them by Susanne at 8:33 A.M. Saturday morning.

"We reconnected the email and I was kind of blown away that the top message was from Susanne Zantop. It was not a personal message. It was a political action message sent out to her network of people who would want to be kept current," recalled Audrey. The message was a request for friends to email their senators and oppose President Bush's choice of John Ashcroft to be US Attorney General. "We felt like telling everyone in a sense, 'Don't send flowers, send an email to your senator, that is sort of what they would want,' " Audrey said.

In addition to voting for more liberal candidates who espoused their ideals, the Zantops were determined to try to fold their idealism into their daily lives.

"They were devoted to their students, and gave time-and-a-half to any student. Extremely generous of spirit. If anybody was in need of any sort, be it a recent widow, be it a stroke victim, be it someone with a broken leg, be it whatever . . . they would respond to them in terms of companionship, or to bring some sumptuous dish. From the practical to the emotional, they were always ready, and not waiting to be asked, but approaching on their own," Audrey McCollum recalled.

Professor Marianne Hirsch told the Associated Press that the Zantops were always prepared to help others. "They had several elderly couples who they had kind of adopted as surrogate parents they took care of, going to fix things at their houses, inviting them to dinner, doing all the things children should do for their parents," she said. "They did that not just to be altruistic, but because they saw an interesting side to people, and they wanted to be part of their lives. They kind of connected to people in a lot of different ways."

chapter 9

At their home in Etna, the Zantops loved the tranquillity of their wooded surroundings, but at the same time they enjoyed frequently filling the house with friends whom they dazzled with stimulating discussions of national and global politics and their interest in the scientific and moral issues of the day.

In the wake of their deaths, friend after friend of the Zantops would recall the efforts the couple had made to welcome them into their home over the years, and the wonderful food from around the world that always appeared when Susanne was cooking.

Susanne liked to wear batik skirts around the house and Half would lounge in cargo shorts and Birkenstocks while they cooked, listed to NPR, and read. Friends hardly ever remember a television running in the home.

The Zantops clearly loved having people over and the rituals that went with being gracious hosts. They were always offering their guests coffee before dinner, or Half's special margaritas during the meal, and espresso afterwards. People left the house uplifted and would talk about the conversations they had at the Zantops' around their offices the next day.

Professor Alexis Jetter described the Zantops' hospitality as an extension of their personalities. "They were more than exceptional, they were magical people," she said.

Like so many others who had been their guests, Professor Birnie commented on the Zantops' love of gourmet food. "When we would go to their house they always had lovely, sort of international kinds of foods. The food preparation was wonderful. I remember the first day they came to the college after they arrived in Montreal. In Hanover that night we were just going to do an American barbecue for them and we had hamburgers and French fries and so forth. Later when I saw how well they cooked themselves I joked that was probably the first—and the last—hamburger and French fries they had in the United States.

"They were known for delicious food and conversation and good wine as well," Birnie said. "They are people with whom you love to talk and learn. You wouldn't go to their house and play charades—you'd be there and be talking. Many of their social friends were on the humanities side of the spectrum."

The Zantops had made a life for themselves out on Trescott Road that immersed them in the natural world surrounding their house.

They grew their own vegetables in a plot in the meadow and made their own jams and jellies with the gooseberry and currant bushes they had transplanted nearby. They planted brilliant bunches of peonies and hostas around the house and the driveway and in the winter they cut out through the cross-country ski trails that ringed their land.

"Their house is very much a part of the outdoors around it. I think they loved the outlook on the meadow, the forests surrounding the meadow, and the long view toward the Green Mountains," Audrey McCollum said.

"There are an extraordinary number of critters. They had a large vegetable garden and they had kind of a tug of war between their love of wildlife and their love of vegetables. They were always negotiating that," she laughed.

"They would sit out there on summer evenings with a sense of tranquillity. One of their many other sides was this attunement to nature. They often sat up here with us in the evening both kind of soaking up the environs but also talking perhaps about global warming," Audrey continued.

Sometimes the couples would watch herds of deer stroll through the fields, other times they would spot the neighborhood's lone little black bear scampering away from the bird feeders.

Half would know when the major annual meteor showers were taking place and the couples would gather on their porches in the late evening with a bottle of the Zantops' favorite V&F. Gonzalez pale dry sherry and watch the light show overhead in the pristine Etna night sky.

The McCollums and the Zantops traded videotapes of tennis matches that they both followed keenly and passed articles about global warming back and forth. But always the McCollums would call first before dropping over because of the Zantops' busy schedule, knowing that if they didn't find them at home they risked tripping their alarm system.

"Half had a very keen analytic mind. As a geologist he had a very long view . . . into millennia. Their interests flowed back and forth in a very unusual way from the ordinary to the minutia of the physical world in which they lived and loved to the most complex political issues to the most esoteric philosophical issues. In a sense they were among the richest people we have known in terms of breadth of interest and depth of knowledge and willingness to say, 'We don't have an answer and let's find one out,' " Audrey said.

"They were multi-faceted people. On the one hand they were intense academics, intense scholars, very accomplished in their field," Audrey continued. "On the other they were hikers, skiers, snowshoers, and sailors.

"They weren't that closely involved in the neighborhood. Their inter-personal world was very much grounded in the college, the students, the faculty, the administrators. They threw themselves into that with such enthusiasm and interest and passion that they didn't have much energy left over," Audrey said.

"They weren't out around the neighborhood except to walk and they were avid walkers. They were out on the road very often because at some times that's the only place you can walk. They did a two-mile loop not uncommonly. In the summer they were avid mushroom collectors and we had silent competitions," she laughed.

"They had a strong circle of friends. They had a very broad range of friends in terms of those who were not native to the United States. They had guests a lot and were guests a lot . . . They shared child raising with each other and other people who had kids their age, so there were a lot of people who grew up around here with Half taking care of them after school," Duncan said.

"Their home was really a gathering place for all kinds of people," Jetter continued. "They were both frighteningly efficient, but with enormous grace and warmth and style. If you can combine that sort of German precision with this wonderful emanating warmth and grace and humor. They were both extremely funny, and put you right at ease. They were both highly regarded in their fields."

"She was fierce and funny and passionate and irreverent and perhaps the best cook I have ever known," Orleck said, blinking away tears. "She was famous for her paella and for her tortes, which were unbelievable. She was the kind of person who embraced you immediately and wanted one person that she loved to meet another. She built a community. She helped not only her friends, but helped other people to become friends. She did so much to sustain this community."

Each July the Zantops would leave for three weeks in Maine where they stayed in a cedar-shingled cabin called The Maples at the Hiram Blake Camp, a small summer-cottage community on a remote little cove called Cape Rosier off Penobscot Bay.

Friends in Maine would marvel at the Zantops' seemingly endless energy as they rose at dawn and paddled out to nearby islands to gather gooseberries and mushrooms. Susanne would turn the berries into preserves and share them around with the other vacationers, and Half would sauté up large piles of chanterelle mushrooms along with fresh hand-raked mussels during impromptu clambakes on the nearby beaches.

The Zantops had a little 14-foot Laser sailboat that he and his daughters became experts at guiding around the coves. In recent years the Zantops and another couple had also bought a cabin cruiser that they rode out through the bay to range up and down the Maine coast from Brunswick to Buck's Harbor.

Close friend Jim Zien's last memories of the Zantops in Maine at the conclusion of their summer 2000 vacation would be of Half, car loaded and ready to go for the return journey to Hanover, kneeling down with his Swiss Army knife and patiently explaining to a child how to distinguish the various minerals in some interesting rocks that had been found on the shoreline.

chapter 10

While detectives continued the clinical, and somewhat cynical, process of examining underneath the surface of someone else's lives looking for any flaws, anything unusual, any twists and coincidences that would stand out only in hindsight, the Zantops' very real lives and deaths had collided hard with those of their daughters,—their extended family in Germany, and their friends and colleagues at Dartmouth and around the world.

The Zantop daughters were the first to arrive back in Hanover.

Dr. Veronika Zantop, 29, flew back in from Seattle, where she was taking a family medicine residency at the University of Washington after having graduated from the University of California at San Francisco in June. Before that she had attended Brown University and had been a research assistant at Harvard.

Mariana Zantop, 27, arrived back in Hanover from New York, where she was enrolled as a graduate student at Columbia University after attending Haverford College. Mariana already had a master's degree in public health from the college, and had spent quite a bit of time in Africa and Central America pursuing a career as an international aid worker.

Because their parents' house was still being methodically processed by the Major Crimes Unit, the Zantop daughters were unable to return home even if they had wanted to. The girls were immediately taken in by close friends.

"Veronika is rather more outgoing than Mariana," said Audrey McCollum. "Mariana is very shy, very quiet-spoken. She and I had developed a certain kind of closeness

because she acted as a reader for a book I published a year
and a half ago. A very clear thinker, very direct, very hon-
est, but always in a tactful way. She's very interested in
other cultures," Audrey noted.

Soon, a dozen other members of the family began arriving from Germany and Spain, including Joachim and Marianne Korsukewitz, Susanne's elderly parents, and four of
Half's sisters. Well-dressed, largely wearing black, and
keeping a low profile, the family members checked quietly
into the Hanover Inn and could be seen walking around the
town and the snow-covered campus in the days leading up
to the memorial service on Saturday, February 3.

Professor Birnie hosted Half's family during the days
pre- ceding the memorial service. "They are sharp, delight-
ful, educated, entertaining people . . . in other words, just
like Half," Birnie said. "They are international people, articulate in multiple languages about world affairs and so
forth, and even into outdoor adventuring. I was chatting
with one of them about a ten-day canoe trip they had just
taken in the Canadian Rockies. They are well traveled in a
variety of circles."

On Monday, January 29, the Zantops' daughters contacted the local Rand–Wilson Funeral Home in Hanover
and made arrangements to have them retrieve their parents'
bodies from the morgue in Concord. The Zantops' remains
were cremated that Friday ahead of the memorial service
that would take place on Saturday.

Hanover Police Chief Nick Giaccone, a nearly thirty-
year veteran of the Hanover department, stepped forward
to help the distraught young women through what was going to follow. Police, especially those who had been to the
house and seen the bodies, had the deepest sympathy for
the Zantop daughters and the traumatization they had experienced, but at the same time there was so much they
hoped the girls could tell them that might shed light on
what had happened.

One of the principal things concerning investigators was
the contents of the house as they were found on the evening

of January 27. It wasn't immediately clear whether anything had been removed by the killers. Perhaps there had been some item or some piece of information the Zantops had in their possession that the killers wanted desperately to gain or recover.

Equally important, detectives wanted to know if anything they had come across in the main portion of the house or in the study didn't belong there and might have been introduced to the scene by the killers.

Police asked Dartmouth staff and the construction workers who were carrying out renovations to the large five-story glass-walled atrium at Fairchild Hall, the building where Half had his office and classrooms, if anyone was missing any tools. They also asked whether Half would have been expected to have had a syringe in his home first-aid kit, and if he would have been expected to store rope or any rock-cutting tools and equipment at his home as part of his geology studies. Police would not comment on their reasons for asking, but reporters took it to mean that all of those things had been found at the Zantop residence, probably in the study.

Police offered to retrieve anything the daughters felt they needed from the house, provided it was cleared with the Major Crimes Unit before it was actually removed. In addition to the daughters, police began walking certain friends of the Zantops through the house because they had been there more recently and might be able to spot anything missing or unusual. Several friends were also asked to voluntarily submit to fingerprinting so their prints could be eliminated from among the "prints of interest" that investigators had found around the home.

Among those who volunteered their prints were the McCollums, who were now wrestling not only with the fact that their friends had been killed in a brutal double murder right next door, but also with the realization that it was they who had encouraged the Zantops to move into the Etna neighborhood in the first place.

Beginning in earnest in the 1980s and continuing through the present day, more and more houses are being built on newly added roads through the woods and hills clustered around Etna. The Zantops' home, constructed in 1985, is one of these recent additions, and by January 2001 there were fifty residences, most of them modern homes on densely wooded three-acre lots, within a half mile of their house.

The Zantops' contemporary home had been commissioned by Thomas and Katharine Almy, who were close friends of the McCollums. The Almys hired architect and novelist Don Metz, well known locally for the series of energy-efficient underground homes he designed around the region in the 1970s, to draw up their new house at 115 Trescott.

"It was a charming little house," recalled Katharine Almy, who is now eighty-five years old. "It was modern, but not extreme."

With its grayish board-and-batten wood siding and the darker gray standing-seam metal roof that sloped out in various sections over the first floor, the house was not startling from the outside, but inside it had a contemporary natural stone and wood theme which fit in well with the north woods environment.

By 1991 the Almys decided to move to a new retirement community called Kendal that was under construction closer to downtown Hanover. At the same time, the Zantops had sent both daughters off to college and were looking to buy a home farther out in the countryside. "Even though Hanover is relatively rural, they wanted more rural," Audrey said.

The McCollums saw the obvious overlapping interests and introduced the two couples. "They hit it right off immediately," Audrey said. "The Zantops loved the house at first sight. The sale went through quite quickly."

"They were lovely people and we were very fond of them," agreed Katharine Almy.

The Zantops made several modifications to the interior of the house, adding lots of built-in cabinetry to the living room, including a special area for Susanne's piano, and having more bookshelves built into the study, along with a large set of desk-like workstations for their computers and office equipment against the wall facing the front driveway.

"It was beautiful. They had very excellent taste and they put in a lot of natural wood," remembered Katharine Almy. "It was greatly improved, the atmosphere was very different than when it was with us. They had brilliant colors in their wall hangings and pictures. Just very clean lines and in very good taste. They had a lot of things they had collected from around the world on the walls. It was just a very attractive house. They were of German origin and they were very precise. Everything was very neat."

The Zantops would invite the Almys and their daughter Susan, the local state representative for Grafton County, back to the house for tea whenever the peonies that Thomas Almy had first planted there were in full bloom.

"They loved to garden and hike and things like that. We used to go over there when the garden was at its best, and they would give us bunches of flowers," Katharine said. "The drainage from the house went down through pipes and into this little pond. It was very small but they always had frogs and goldfish there."

The pond and most of the other features around the house were completely obscured by a thick blanket of snow when the murders took place in late January. Detectives in snowshoes worked their way around the property and trekked amongst the woods looking for any sign of evidence, perhaps a weapon that had been thrown from the house, the driveway, or the nearby road.

Officers also searched through barns and sheds behind several nearby houses, but didn't seem to find anything of interest.

In the summer, residents would be startled one morning when the Hanover officers and state troopers returned in force to spend the day walking shoulder-to-shoulder in a long line along the road and through the meadows for a quarter mile in all directions around the house. Police explained that it was just a precautionary check to make sure that there was nothing that had been missed during the wintertime searches.

One point about the Zantops and their house that the McCollums and others sought to clarify in the month following the killings was the initial notion that there had been renters or other strangers staying on the property.

No one stayed at the house who wasn't a friend of the couple, and their considerable altruistic instincts were largely devoted to people whom they already knew, friends explained.

"A few years ago, Bosnian refugees were coming to the north country, and I remember that Half offered landscaping work to the man who I think was actually a professional, but who had no way to establish or earn an income here. People coming from Europe in states of need they would reach out to," Audrey McCollum said.

Bob McCollum added, "I don't think there was any sort of regularity or pattern other than that the people they shared their home with and invited over were for the most part friends, or people that they knew well that were in need, or whatever."

As an example, Audrey pointed to Roxana Verona, saying, "They were very close friends, shaped in part by the fact that about two years ago she became widowed and one of their endearing characteristics is to reach out to somebody who's in intense personal distress. They had her over every week or two for a meal, most particularly on weekends when she would be missing her husband the most. It was very informal."

The Zantops seemed to feel that houses remained spiritually attached to their owners even after they moved. Just as they had kept in contact with the Almys over the years, they made it a point to keep up a relationship with the person to whom they had sold their old house on Woodmore Road. That person was Roxana Verona.

chapter 11

In the week after the bodies were discovered, over thirty full-time investigators were assigned to the case, most of those from the New Hampshire State Police and the Attorney General's Office.

Hanover Police Chief Nick Giaccone offered non-stop overtime to any of his officers who wanted to come in and put in additional shifts working on the case.

An upstairs conference room in the Hanover Public Safety Building was converted to a "war room" to manage the case, and was staffed around the clock. Six additional phone lines were run in to help detectives working the case and a series of daily briefings were held to keep investigators up to speed on the information that was being gathered. Eventually the FBI would send along technicians who would set up a "lead management system" called Rapid Start there in the Hanover war room.

The Rapid Start computers are designed to help in high-profile investigations that take in enormous amounts of stray tips, leads, and details collected by investigators. The relational databases that Rapid Start uses can spot patterns and minute connections that harried detectives might otherwise overlook. Something as seemingly insignificant as two otherwise unconnected subjects being interviewed months apart in different states by different detectives, but using the exact same word to describe an item or an occurrence would be the type of clue that Rapid Start would notice.

Detectives started in immediately on the enormous amount of interviews that needed to be done with close friends and associates of the Zantops while still others started trying to piece together the leads that were being phoned in from literally across the world. Most of the phone calls contributed information about the Zantops' lives, especially their movements in the weeks preceding their deaths, but for all of the activity, there weren't many of the kinds of "hot tips" that fill up television police dramas.

There were a few brief flurries of activity during the first couple of days. When what appeared to be a bloody hand-print was found on a chair in the basement kitchen area of the Massachusetts Hall dormitory, troopers swooped in, but soon said that it was unrelated to the investigation.

Employees discovered a bloody T-shirt in a Dumpster behind Doug's Exit 19 Sunoco station off Interstate 89 about seven miles from the Zantops' residence on Wednesday, January 31. Police came in, took the shirt, and searched the rest of the Dumpster, but didn't appear to feel it was linked to the Zantop case.

In the offices of the German Department on the third floor of the ornate old Dartmouth Hall building, parts of which date back to 1784, the small conference room outside Susanne's office had become an impromptu memorial. Floral arrangements were arrayed next to boxes of German chocolates that friends sent to her colleagues along with cards and letters of condolence. A single pink rose sat on the floor in a vase directly in front of her wooden office door, which had been locked and ordered sealed by the police. On the door, Susanne's academic conference schedules remained taped with a few small cartoons and yellowed German newspaper clippings of poems.

As the days went by, detectives combed through the Zantops' sealed offices on the campus, and requested all the teacher evaluation forms that had been filled out by their students for the past two years running.

Three days after the bodies were discovered, Detective Robert Eastabrook of the Major Crimes Unit computer crimes section executed a search warrant on the Dartmouth College computer network. Detectives removed the college's computers from Half's office in Fairchild Hall and from Susanne's office in Dartmouth Hall, and then went over to the main email servers at the brand-new Barry Library building. There, Dartmouth computer technician David Gelhar provided Eastabrook with copies of a special backup of the Zantops' email directories that had been made shortly after the college learned they had been killed.

Police also executed warrants on the regional telephone company requesting months' worth of the Zantops' phone records.

Investigators wouldn't tell reporters what the computer, mail server, and phone searches did or didn't reveal, but the guess in the press corps was that not much of value was learned, since none of the significant developments in the case over the weeks that followed ever seemed to be linked to email or other computer connections.

One of the more unusual features of the first week of the investigation was the message being sent out to the public by the New Hampshire Attorney General's Office. Officials were telling reporters that no arrests were imminent, and that little, if anything, was known about why the Zantops had been killed. At the same time, police were telling neighbors on Trescott Road not to be unduly alarmed, and Hanover Police Chief Nick Giaccone even admonished the press for alarming the town.

"The community is concerned with the sensationalism that you've created here," Giaccone lectured the dozen television cameras in front of him. He said that local children had been scared by the media coverage, and added, "There is no bogey man under their bed or in their closet."

All of this seemed to suggest that police actually did have some idea that at the very least, the Zantops had been the specific target of whatever had happened in their study, and the public at large was not at risk. But when pressed to explain, officials were hedging that concept as well.

"If we had specific reliable information to believe that the community would be at risk, then we would express that, because that would be our duty," Attorney General McLaughlin said. "At the present time we simply do not have sufficient information, sufficient understanding of the facts surrounding this case, to cause us to make any statements," he continued. "On the one hand, we do not want to be alarmist. On the other hand, we do not want to treat this situation in a way which understates its importance. Obviously there has been an exceedingly tragic event in this community and we are working diligently to pursue the evidence," he concluded.

So little information was given out at the daily briefings that the press corps began referring to the Assistant Attorney General who briefed the media as "Kelly 'No Comment' Ayotte." The frustration level amongst both the public and, especially, the press began to rise with each passing daily briefing from officials. Reporters were used to having investigators withhold certain details in ongoing investigations, but nothing like this. After the student reporters had seen several of the press conferences in action, the joke around *The Dartmouth*'s offices was that they were surprised that police had even confirmed it was the Zantops that had been killed.

The larger press corps' view of the investigators was getting so down that troopers felt compelled to start mentioning in the hallways that Kelly Ayotte was really a nice person if you got to know her, and that she was even known to wear jeans to parties and drink beer. The press from Boston and New York began to wonder if they'd left the country and wandered into the Twilight Zone.

Suddenly on Wednesday, January 31, a genuine break seemed to appear in the case, and a palpable thrill shivered through the press corps that had assembled in Hanover.

A television station in Derry, New Hampshire, caught wind of the fact that investigators from the Hanover Homicide Task Force had impounded a white Daewoo rental car that had been turned back in at the Manchester Airport with what appeared to be bloodstains in the trunk.

"They searched the car and fingerprinted it," Thrifty Car Rental employee Young Kim told WNDS television, adding, "They didn't want us to go near it, but as far as I know from my supervisors, it's connected to the Dartmouth murders."

Employees remembered that the car had been driven by a middle-aged man from Arizona who had been going to the Hanover area for the weekend. They said there had been a business card from Arizona State University found in the car, along with a pair of eyeglasses. Both items had been turned over to police.

The card belonged to Stanley N. Williams, a forty-eight-year-old volcanologist at ASU, and there were enough connections between him and Half Zantop to send a half-dozen New Hampshire investigators, including Kelly Ayotte, heading right for the airport to follow him out to Phoenix for a closer look.

Stanley Williams had attended Dartmouth and received his doctorate in Earth Sciences there in 1983. Professor Dick Stoiber had supervised his doctoral dissertation and Williams certainly knew Half Zantop and most of the other members of Dartmouth's Earth Sciences Department well.

Williams had taught at Arizona State University since 1991, and had been a professor of Volcanology since 1995. He had also taught at Dartmouth in 2000 as a visiting professor.

Williams' wife Lynda had graduated from Dartmouth in 1984, a year after Stanley, and Half Zantop had been the advisor on her master's degree in Geology. Lynda Williams now worked as a faculty researcher for the Solid State Science Center at ASU.

Susanne Zantop also had a connection to Arizona State University. She served on the editorial board of a publication called the *German Studies Review* which was put out by the German Studies Association based at ASU in

Tempe, Arizona. She had been to a conference in Houston with members of the association in October 2000, and had emailed the editor of the *Review* a day or two before she was killed regarding a manuscript she was looking over for them.

Stanley Williams was actually well known not just in the Earth Sciences Departments at ASU and Dartmouth, but throughout the worldwide scientific community because of his connection to one of the deadliest disasters in modern science.

As Dartmouth Earth Sciences Professor Jim Aronson noted, "Stanley's a very famous person. He's somewhat of a legend."

Williams was the leader of a 1993 expedition to study a volcano called Galeras in Colombia that had been threatening to erupt. The basic purpose of the expedition was to see if a team of scientists with several different specializations could accurately predict an eruption. The short answer was that they couldn't. Six scientists and three tourists were killed when Galeras blew, and Williams himself was severely injured in the massive eruption.

Several aspects of the expedition's decision to ascend the Galeras volcano on the day of the eruption were controversial within the scientific community, and there were those who blamed Williams for overlooking data that they thought should have dissuaded him from taking the team up to the crater.

In January, when the Zantops were murdered, the publishing world was aware that there were two separate books about the Galeras tragedy due in bookstores over the summer.

The first was by science journalist Victoria Bruce, who has a master's degree in Geology, and whose book *No Apparent Danger* argued that Williams failed to read seismic data on the morning of the eruption that could have saved the lives of those lost in the expedition. Bruce's book was also going to allege that Williams had gone around after the eruption claiming to be the "lone survivor" of the blast, when in fact other scientists, including some who were actually closer to the crater than he was at the time, had also survived.

While this less-than-flattering account of Williams' role in the expedition was being prepared for print, Williams was busy co-authoring his own account of the expedition called *Surviving Galeras* in which he and several other prominent volcanologists argued that there was no way that he could have foreseen the eruption.

Half Zantop was not mentioned in either book, and sources familiar with Williams' manuscript said that even though Half sometimes dabbled in volcanology, he had never been approached to participate in, nor been asked to endorse, Williams' book. Aside from his arrival and departure from Hanover, which bracketed the time of the murders, and his general association with the victims, there didn't appear to be any specific reason to suspect Williams of any involvement in the killings; however, employees of rental car agencies throughout the state had been asked to be on the lookout for anything unusual in returning cars, especially cars that had been to the Hanover area. There was something in the trunk of the white Daewoo that struck the employees as alarming: a cardboard box that appeared to have a bloodstain on the bottom.

When the New Hampshire detectives arrived in Arizona, they interviewed both of the Williamses in their home. Stanley and Lynda told investigators that Stanley had been back at Dartmouth to attend Dick Stoiber's 90th birthday party in neighboring Norwich, Vermont. It was the same party that Half Zantop had been planning to duck out and briefly attend on the evening of the day that he was murdered.

Stanley told the authorities that he had actually made several trips back to New Hampshire and Vermont in the past few months because Stoiber's health was clearly failing, and there were research projects that both men had

worked on together which they were rushing to complete
ahead of the inevitable. (In fact, Stoiber would die of natural causes just days later on February 9.)

When he learned on Sunday, along with much of the
rest of the campus, that Half and Susanne were dead, Williams had attended a support meeting that was called for
the stunned members of the Earth Sciences Department that
afternoon, and decided to extend his stay for a couple of
days.

In addition to a detailed account of his movements during the days he was in the Northeast, the detectives were
especially interested in learning what Stanley had to say
about the cardboard box that had been found in the trunk
of the rented Daewoo at the Manchester Airport. What, they
wanted to know, were the odd stains that looked like blood
on the bottom of the box?

"Moose stew," Stanley explained.

The nephew of one of Stoiber's home health care pro-
viders, with whom Williams had become friendly, had recently shot a moose, and on that Monday night, two days
after the murders, Stanley Williams had picked up a pot of
fresh moose stew from them and taken it to another friend's
residence for dinner. Along the way, some of the stew
spilled out of the pot and into the box.

Detectives called back to the New Hampshire State Police Forensics Laboratory, which confirmed that initial tests
showed that whatever was in the box wasn't human blood.

After cross-checking the Williamses' alibis and explanations, the investigators were satisfied and headed back to
the airport in Phoenix. When she returned to the next press
briefing at the Hanover Police Department, Kelly Ayotte
confirmed that she had gone to Arizona with the others.
"We were there for several days. What I can say is that
those individuals [in Arizona] aren't being treated as suspects," Ayotte told the briefing.

Weeks later, Lynda Williams would write an indignant
letter to *The Dartmouth* explaining about the moose stew

stain and accusing the media, including her alma mater's student paper, of "irresponsible speculation and innuendo."

In her letter, Williams described how, after she and her husband were questioned by "respectful and intelligent" investigators and had "cooperated fully," she subsequently decided to tell each reporter who called, wondering why homicide detectives had impounded her husband's rental car and flown halfway across the nation to talk with him, that she had no comment.

With two unsolved murders still under investigation, Williams decried the fact that reporters had called her at work, and then called other ASU professors at home, once she had refused to speak with the press.

What Lynda Williams failed to note was that the other professors, her campus police force, the regular police in Tempe, and detectives with the Arizona State Police were actually taking those calls from reporters and patiently explaining what little they knew of events, and largely saying that Stanley Williams seemed like a nice guy who was unlikely to be mixed up in a murder.

Unfortunately, the only people who weren't busy defending the Williamses were the Williamses, and, operating on the simple principle that people who hide from the press may have a reason to do so, reporters continued asking questions and watching and waiting for the Williamses to surface. In her letter, Williams complained that, after she had disconnected her home phone, reporters started showing up in her driveway. They were probably having difficulty calling her.

"Because of a moose stew stain, you have slandered my husband's work, insinuated he was a suspect in murder, and accused me of having an affair with my advisor. Your stories have sickened us and caused heartache for our teenaged children. There is no excuse," Lynda Williams wrote to *The Dartmouth*, continuing, "Yet a retraction has not been published. The readers will only know of the accusations. They will never consider our innocence and the abuse that reporters inflicted on us and undoubtedly many others. The irony of this is that Stan has always championed speaking to the press as a necessity for our democracy."

The irony of that was, if Lynda and Stanley Williams had spoken to the press in the first place, they probably could have avoided the insinuations and inferences that the public and the press supposedly drew from their behavior.

Once the brief flurry of activity centered around Arizona subsided, the Zantop investigation once again focused back on the Dartmouth campus, and at the end of the first week, Attorney General McLaughlin stepped back up to the podium at the daily press briefing and finally confirmed how the Zantops had been killed.

"The deaths were in fact caused by stabbing," McLaughlin said.

He then gave reporters their first real insight into the investigation's thinking to date about the possible scenario surrounding the double murders.

"Conceding that this may have been a random event," he began, "it seems to us that the logic of the situation is different, and the logic points us in the direction of saying that some person either went there with the purpose of harming the Zantops, or went there with some other purpose and, while there, something occurred to cause that person or persons to harm the Zantops," the attorney general continued.

"We are probably dealing with a more targeted event than a random event. On balance, we don't believe that it is random. The other side of this is, since we don't know that it wasn't random, I don't want to tell the community it wasn't random. I'd rather have the community listen to an intelligent discussion than deal in these black-and-white ways. This is a community that is used to intelligent discussion, quite literally, and one of the issues that we have here is that it is very frustrating for folks who live in this environment to hear us declare conclusions to them. This is literally a community who has thousands of people who are acculturated to ask detailed questions, and they feel frustrated when they don't get answers from us. We appreciate and respect that, and we are trying to deal as accurately as we can," McLaughlin said.

McLaughlin downplayed, but did not entirely rule out, suggestions in *The Dartmouth* that a ritual killing of some sort might be involved. Basically, he said that one person's ritual might be hard to interpret, but that there were no overt symbols or anything like that left at the scene.

McLaughlin also said that the investigation was getting tremendous cooperation from the Hanover community. "We gain greater and greater insight into the lives of these very private people, and greater and greater insight causes us to ask other questions, ultimately with the goal of solving this crime," he said.

Asked how he thought the case was really going, and if there would be an arrest soon, McLaughlin replied, "We're eternally optimistic. Given the resources we have here, the person who did this, who may well be watching this, should take no comfort in the fact that they have not yet been apprehended," McLaughlin said, and then, looking pointedly straight at the bank of television cameras arrayed in front of him, he added, "Be patient. We'll be there."

chapter 12

The week after the murders was one of intense police work, but also one of intense mourning at Dartmouth.

There was an impromptu gathering at one of the college chapels on Sunday night, and two hundred people, many of them weeping, gathered Monday for "a hug and some tea" at the home of Dartmouth President James Wright near the center of the college. On Thursday a regularly scheduled "Community Hour" luncheon turned into a discussion of the Zantop situation.

All across the campus, feelings of grief mixed with fear and confusion as Dartmouth wondered if someone still in their midst had carried out the crime; and always, the question of "Why?" hung over every discussion.

Nancy Crumbine, a professor with the English and Education Department, spoke as she left the Community Hour, saying, "We are all just waiting, and we are trying to be patient, and we are trying not to let our imaginations go wild, and we are all just so grief-stricken.

"Everybody is pitching in and doing what they can to try and help each other through this. The mood was very quiet and pensive," Crumbine said. "I just wanted to be around other people who are going through this. President Wright just thanked everybody for their cooperation and said this was an impossible situation and we were all coping with it well. The most important thing was the sense of community. The college is really unified in their grief."

The next day President Wright spoke to journalists at a press conference at the Hanover Inn. He tried to reassure parents of Dartmouth students around the world that the college was being vigilant about safety and coping with the tragedy.

Although always dignified and thoughtful, Wright is something of an anomaly amongst the small private club of Ivy League presidents. As a younger man he served in the Marine Corps and became a coal miner in Illinois before the stories the miners told of their history prompted him to enroll in college at the age of 21. He had come to Dartmouth in 1969 as a History professor and worked his way up through the administration to lead the school.

In a dark suit that accentuated his white hair, Wright leaned heavily on the podium, faced the reporters arrayed in the lobby before him, and began in a sad voice, "We would just as soon these circumstances hadn't drawn you here.

"I have been at Dartmouth for thirty-two years," Wright continued. "I have lived for probably twenty of those thirty-two years out in Etna, in fact, for several years I lived very close to the Zantops. They were friends, they were neighbors, they were people I enjoyed very much as colleagues," Wright said. "We know we are quite privileged to have a college in a quiet, special place. It's a place where people really have a sense of confidence, of optimism, of security, a sense of belonging that I think has been terribly important to Dartmouth. Obviously events such as this shatter for many that sense of optimism, of confidence, of security."

Wright also obliquely acknowledged the spotlight of suspicion that was glaring down on everyone who might have known the Zantops as the investigation searched for connections and possible motives. "A community like ours has to find spaces to grieve, and it's hard for us to do that with the questions that remain outstanding," Wright said, adding, "A terrible thing happened to us, and we can't allow something that was vicious and unnatural to come to characterize our relationships with each other."

Even though the police were downplaying the chances of additional violence, Dartmouth moved swiftly to try to reassure students and parents that there was additional security on the campus.

"It's hard to feel secure when something terrible has happened, and we simply have to acknowledge that. We don't know anything, and I think it is the mystery of this, trying to understand something that is not understandable in the best of circumstances, and then having pieces of it that are not clear, so I'm not surprised that people somehow feel different, that they feel less secure and less safe, and I think we have to try to support them, and we have to try to move through this," Wright said.

James Larimore, Dean of Student Life and Security, echoed Wright, saying, "Times such as these test the strength and character of any community. It is hard to imagine any set of circumstances any more difficult than the one we now face."

The college police began offering those students and staff who were used to walking around the campus a twenty-four-hour ride service to anywhere they needed to go around Dartmouth, and they added a hotline for concerned parents and friends to call for information. Uniformed Department of Safety and Security personnel, normally rather low-key around the college, began to increase their visibility to provide some reassurance.

"Groups of students and groups of faculty got together in their homes and were there for each other," said Dr. Mark Reed, Dartmouth's Director of Counseling Services. "People are really responding with profound disbelief. It's clear to me that the Zantops were universally cherished and loved."

When what normally would have been the Zantops' classroom hours came around again on the schedules, counselors went and sat in with the badly shaken students.

"Sitting in the classroom that Professor Zantop was teaching at, it was just difficult for students to believe that he wasn't there. Over the course of the next days and weeks, we are going to be trying to help them get through this," Reed said. "It will come in a number of waves of sadness and disbelief, but the support they've had from each other has been impressive."

While the campus reeled from its loss, the investigation continued apace, mostly behind the scenes, but the public would get occasional glimpses of the activity. On Saturday, February 3, exactly one week after the murders, Hanover police and state troopers set up a small roadblock a couple of houses down Trescott from the Zantop residence. Every car coming through in both directions was flagged down, their license numbers recorded, and their drivers asked if they regularly traveled that route on Saturdays, and if they had, had they noticed anything, anything at all, seven days before?

While the police roadblock was looking for information from drivers in Etna, back in Hanover, nine hundred students, colleagues, friends, and relatives of the Zantops were gathering around the Green for their memorial service.

The ruddy red-pink granite Rollins Chapel building with its distinctive single turret sits almost exactly between Half and Susanne's offices on the campus, and streams of mourners, most in dark full-length winter dress coats, made their way from both directions carrying bunches of flowers as they converged on Rollins at two o'clock. Photographers and camera crews on a large platform set up across the street began beaming the Zantops' memorial live across the region.

The service was conducted in English and German for the benefit of the dozen Zantop relatives who had traveled from Germany, Spain, or Corsica for the memorial.

"Our hearts ache in the loss, and we have questions and seek answers that may never come," said Reverend Gwendolyn King as the service began.

College President James Wright was the first to speak to those packing Rollins Chapel, saying, "Susanne and Half joyfully embraced life and people. They were gifted educators and mentors, respected scholars, and for so many of us, moral exemplars of considered lives well lived. Individuals to be sure, each unique and special, but who could think of one without thinking of the other?

"We share a profound gratitude for Susanne's bracing energy and honesty, for Half's quiet listening and smiling responses, and for the beauty and the goodness of the life they made together," Wright said.

"Half and Susanne modeled the kind of people we would like to be. They opened their hearts, sharing their zest for conversation and delicious food, their enthusiasm for knowledge and for sharing it, their pleasure in the sight of grazing deer, their joy in the rigor of an afternoon of cross-country skiing. They gardened and they sailed, they entertained friends, students, colleagues, and guest scholars, they cared passionately about the world beyond our campus and participated actively in debate about national and international issues. We learned much from their lives and we benefit, and we must continue to benefit, from their challenge to be the very best that they knew we could be," Wright said.

After hymns were sung and candles lit, and colleagues and friends had spoken movingly of the Zantops' broad interests, myriad friendships, and devotion to teaching and scholarship, the podium was taken by Dr. Sujee Fonseca of Toronto, who wore a simple white sari to the service. Originally from Sri Lanka, Fonseca had been a student at Dartmouth when she ran into immigration problems with the United States that nearly derailed her dream of becoming a doctor. Hearing of her dilemma, the Zantops had practically adopted Fonseca, paying her way through medical school in Canada, and referring to her as their "third daughter."

Fonseca choked back tears as she told the gathered mourners of an interaction she witnessed at the Zantops' home on December 28, when Susanne broke a cherished Christmas ornament. "Susanne came up to Half with a broken ornament in hand and pouted lips and said, 'Half, would you please put this together?' and Half said, "Susanne, nothing is permanent, my dear, except my love for you."

As the assembled mourners filed out along the Hanover Green to the Hopkins Center for a reception following the service, President Wright paused to reflect on the week-long investigation into the Zantops' deaths.

"So much of the focus over the past week has been on the manner of their death, and I think what we said today was that we have to look at them and the measure of their life and the manner of their life. That's what these friends meant to us and that's what our focus was on today," said Wright.

"I think that we all know that what happened out there that night and who did it is an important part of resolution, but we have lost two friends, and knowing what happened to them is not going to bring them back. It is not the nature of their death, but the manner of their life that is so important to those of us who knew them," Wright concluded.

Following the memorial service, Veronika and Mariana Zantop and their aunts, uncles, and grandparents drove the short distance and spent some time in the chapel area of the Rand–Wilson Funeral Home where Half and Susanne's ashes were waiting. After spending some final time together as a group, their parents' ashes were given to the girls, and the small, sad gathering broke up.

The next day was the start of an especially subdued Dartmouth Winter Carnival. On Monday nearly a foot of new snow blanketed New Hampshire and Vermont, and on Tuesday, February 6, the overseas members of the Zantop family assembled mid-day in front of the Hanover Inn for a final round of hugs before their separate bus rides to airports in Boston and Montreal and a series of long flights home.

chapter 13

As the days went by and more interviews by detectives were accomplished, the Hanover Homicide Task Force began to get a better idea of what the Zantops had been doing in the weeks before they died.

The two were always a whirlwind of activity, and details of their movements in the days before they were killed were closely guarded by the investigators.

The Zantops had been German citizens during most of their tenure at Dartmouth, indeed since they were born, and it was only in 1998 that they had become naturalized American citizens.

The couple had told friends at the time that as they became more and more involved in American politics, especially Democratic Party campaigns and issues, they felt they should switch their citizenship over and become voters themselves.

Despite the formal switch in allegiance, the Zantops still remained closely connected with their homeland, and traveled to Germany frequently.

Following a New Year's Eve party at their home on Trescott with a group of their friends, Susanne had left in mid-January for a week-long stay in Berlin to do more research for a German Studies project. When she returned to Hanover she continued working on several writing projects. Half had also recently completed a semester-long program in Berlin.

In the month before his death, Half had been teaching classes several days a week and preparing a revised edition of a geology book he had first published in 1988.

Wednesday, January 24, was Half's sixty-third birthday.

That day Susanne had emailed her friend Susannah Herschel, a professor of Jewish Studies at Dartmouth who was expecting to give birth any day, and invited her over to the Trescott Road house for tea. "I came home after seeing her Wednesday and said to my husband, 'I am so grateful to know her. I just grow from knowing her,' " Herschel later told the *Valley News*.

On Thursday evening the Zantops had gone downtown with Roxana Verona and seen the movie *Crouching Tiger, Hidden Dragon*.

On Friday morning, the day before her death, Susanne came in to work early in the morning, as was her habit. "I saw her Friday morning," said Professor Bruce Duncan. "She usually came in early, and I do too, and we chatted pleasantly and got to work, and I don't even remember what we talked about then," he said.

Professor Richard Birnie last saw Half in Birnie's office in Fairchild Hall on Friday afternoon. Half had sat down next to Birnie's desk and the two men chatted about departmental business. "We were talking about a number of things in the department. I'm the chair, but I'm stepping aside this year and we were talking about who might be the new chair of the department. Half was interested in the next planning phase for the college, and most of the conversation was about that. He was kind of interested in the broader plan for the whole institution, and how it might lead to a capital campaign and so forth," Birnie recalled.

As the work day ended Friday, Professors Marianne Hirsch and Leo Spitzer, a couple who were close friends of Half and Susanne, stopped by the Zantops' house to borrow two extra pairs of snowshoes for friends who were visiting over the weekend.

Hirsch and Spitzer mentioned that they were headed over to see Susannah Herschel, who had just given birth to her daughter.

Susanne decided to join the expedition, and she went to

the attached greenhouse off her living room and selected a pot of little spring daffodils to bring to Professor Herschel.

On the way back from seeing the newborn, Susanne invited Hirsch and Spitzer to join her and Half for dinner. In her usual inimitable style, Susanne set the table with her bright Mexican plates, poured out the wine, and served up sautéed shrimp with garlic, broiled trout, roasted potatoes, asparagus, and salad without any seeming effort.

After dinner, Half whipped up a round of espressos and then the two couples decided to head off to the Hopkins Center on the Hanover Green and see the movie *Best in Show*, a comedy about dog shows.

One of the last Dartmouth students to see the Zantops alive was twenty-one-year-old Meghan Dowd, a senior from Fairfield, Iowa, who had taken Half's Intro to Earth Sciences class during her freshman year.

Dowd was working in the Hopkins Center box office and sold Half and Susanne their tickets to *Best in Show* around 8 P.M. "He was just always a cheerful presence around campus," Dowd said. "He was very witty. He just came in with a lot of energy. He was with it, too. He knew what his students were thinking in class. I found out about the murder through an email Saturday night, when I came home and my roommates told me. It was just completely a shock."

Later in the evening Friday, after the movie, the Zantops and the other two professors parted company, planning to see each other again in just over twenty-four hours, on Sunday morning at a cross-country skiing and snow-shoeing birthday party that Professors Alexis Jetter and Annelise Orleck were throwing for their young daughter.

Saturday, January 27, the day the Zantops were murdered, had only a few specific points of reference that set the timeline for what must have happened.

At 8:33 A.M., Susanne sent out an email to friends on a political mailing list that she maintained on her home office computer in their study. It was the political missive asking friends to oppose the nomination of John Ashcroft to be United States Attorney General.

At around 10:30 A.M., Susanne phoned Roxana Verona and confirmed their plans for dinner at 6:30 P.M., that evening. This was the conversation where Susanne told Roxana to take the unusual step of letting herself in through the unlocked front door.

Over the noon hour, the Zantops traveled the short distance into downtown Hanover and had lunch with another couple at a popular restaurant called Molly's Balloon. Employees told police that the lunch appeared to have been at the invitation of the other unidentified couple, who had picked up the check for all four of them at the end of the meal.

The Zantops returned home early in the afternoon and Susanne at least had already gotten some food out in the kitchen, apparently planning to start cooking some recipes for that evening's dinner with Roxana, when someone appeared at their front doorstep.

Professor Emeritus Dick Stoiber's birthday party began at 5 P.M. in Norwich, Vermont, and as the two hours ticked away, the close-knit gathering began to notice that Half hadn't appeared. "Many of us commented at the party, 'I wonder where Half is?'" Professor Birnie later recalled.

Audrey McCollum's 911 call, just moments after Roxana Verona discovered the bodies, rang in at 6:43 P.M., and the first police officer reached the Zantops' house at 6:53 P.M.

As the day began on Sunday, Jetter and Orleck would have to explain to their daughter, who had put on a special dress that the Zantops had given her as a present earlier, that her German friends would not be coming after all. Instead of snow-shoeing with friends for the day, Jetter and Orleck would stand in the back of the first press briefing, among the televisions and the weight-lifting equipment that had been pushed aside in the Hanover Fire Department's multi-purpose room and watch as police explained to seventy reporters that the investigation into the Zantops' deaths was under way.

chapter 14

As the Zantop investigation entered its second week, little new information filtered out to the press corps except for comments that suggested the investigation was now expanding out beyond the campus into other states and even around the world.

Members of the attorney general's office had repeatedly said that the FBI hadn't been asked to join the case, but they added that the Bureau had been consulted on some matters, and the drift toward the eventual arrival of federal agents seemed inevitable.

Hanover Police Chief Nick Giaccone told reporters that the Zantops had not been the focus of any threats prior to their deaths, and there had never been any interaction between them and the Hanover Police Department that was anything other than routine.

Authorities appealed to the public to continue to call and report anything that may have been seen around Trescott Road in the days surrounding the murders, and Kelly Ayotte answered the same questions day after day with sentences that often began, "As I said on Tuesday . . . ," or, "As the attorney general said on Monday . . ."

Then, mid-week, Ayotte announced that the FBI's help had been requested, specifically because of the Bureau's national and international contacts, which could help in tracking down people the Zantops knew overseas, and with analysis of some of the forensic evidence. Ayotte said that the federal agents would immediately start joining the thirty-five investigators who were already on the case.

"It's been over a week since the Zantops were found

murdered in their home, and the commitment of the state
of New Hampshire to solving this case remains steadfast.
We continue to broaden this investigation in a logical fashion to speak with people who knew the Zantops or who
were known to the Zantops," Ayotte said.

"The FBI is not involved begrudgingly, the FBI is involved at the request of my office, the state police, and the
request of the Hanover Police Department. We are working
as a team, and the dialog between us and the FBI has been
cooperative," Ayotte assured reporters, adding a short time
later, "The focus is not only on Hanover, but also on the
world community. It is not on one to the exclusion of the
other."

Pressed again on whether the community should be taking defensive precautions against a renewed attack by the
killer or killers, Ayotte echoed McLaughlin's remarks of a
few days before.

"The information that the investigation has received
leads us to believe that it was more of a targeted event. We
have not entirely ruled out other possibilities; however, we
are still leaning in the same direction that we spoke of last
week," Ayotte said, adding, "I would hope that the information that we've developed that this is more than likely a
targeted event would give the community some level of
comfort."

After Kelly Ayotte finished, New Hampshire State Police Colonel Gary Sloper also commented on the scope of
the investigation, saying, "We are putting a major manpower thrust into this investigation and will continue to do
so until this matter is solved. This is a very significant effort. We are putting a huge emphasis on working out the
leads and continuing to try and solve this case—as are the
Hanover Police. The efforts are significant. The manpower
commitment is significant."

chapter 15

The rumor mill surrounding the Zantop case was now in full swing, and reporters were taking even small pieces of information, like an unmarked cruiser seen in front of a particular campus building, and wracking their brains trying to figure out what it might mean in the bigger picture.

What little of the investigation the press could see through the cracks in the armor suggested either that investigators were completely stumped, or that there were so many Byzantine twists and turns that investigators were off chasing wild geese.

If a serious suspect wasn't developed soon, reporters joked amongst themselves, eventually, whenever the FBI was called in, they would just hand the case over to the X-Files.

Then, a week into February, the X-Files angle materialized in the form of a man named Archimedes Plutonium.

Mr. Plutonium, or "Arky" as some of his fans around the world affectionately refer to him, is one of those real-life characters who supersede imagination. If a screenwriter made him up, he would be considered too contrived to allow for sufficient suspension of disbelief; however, as a very real person, he was about to have his fifteen minutes of fame as a suspect in the Zantop homicides.

When the first glimmers of the Internet dawned in America in the late 1980s, Archimedes Plutonium (known as Ludwig Poehlmann before he legally changed his name) was in the right place at the right time. Namely, he was behind the sink in the kitchen of the Hanover Inn washing dishes.

Dartmouth was one of the first campuses to have both the vision and the cold hard cash to wire their campus for maximum use of email. Students were required to have their own individual Apple computers back in the days when other colleges were still thinking of getting a few for the library. One of the first widely used email programs, known as "Blitzmail," was developed at Dartmouth, and to this day it remains the backbone of campus life.

As part of the college's early evangelical efforts to make email catch on around the school, Dartmouth gave not only every student and faculty member, but also every college employee their own email account in the ".edu" educational Internet domain. Among those given this small perk were the employees of the Dartmouth-owned Hanover Inn, which sits directly across the Hanover Green from most of the college.

In their wildest megapixel dreams of digital cyber-revolution, the college could never have imagined what an electrifying effect this small homestead on the techno-frontier would have on one lone dishwasher who embraced their behest to him heart and soul.

The forty-something Poehlmann drew little attention to himself as he biked around the Dartmouth campus. He had a distinctive bald head and an engaging grin, but anyone who looked closely at him as he wandered among the stacks in the science libraries would notice that he had written equations in black felt-tip marker all over his ski parka.

At work Poehlmann was an obscure employee who was looking forward to that day, still years away in the distant future, when he would be eligible for recognition at an annual staff dinner for having put in a decade of service at the pot sink without ever having missed a day of work.

However, as a popular cartoon once pointed out, "On the Internet no one knows you're a dog," and with the email address of ArchimedesPlutonium@Dartmouth.edu, the once and former Poehlmann could wade right in amongst the Usenet postings from scientists and universities around the world. For all practical purposes, the name Dartmouth in his on-line address led people to assume that he must be a scientist or researcher there, or at the very least, one of Dartmouth's students.

If Arky posted an observation or asked a question in a discussion group, even if it seemed a little odd, he would frequently get serious responses from scientists at some of the most prestigious government labs and university departments around the planet. After all, in the early days when the Internet was still largely a private playground of the intellectual elite, how nuts could the questions really be if they were coming from someone that Dartmouth College seemingly had trusted with access to their computers?

The answer was actually pretty well full-blown gonzo get-the-net nuts with little colored sprinkles on top.

Among many, many other things, Archimedes Plutonium was convinced that the rest of the scientific community had failed to notice one rather important point: That the entire observable universe is actually the 94th electron of a single plutonium atom.

To correct this oversight, Mr. Plutonium was prepared not only to change his name, but also to post voluminous amounts of material onto the Net . . . several times a day . . . every single day . . . year after year after year. Archimedes Plutonium posted his thoughts, his observations, and his many theories on science and physics bulletin boards, and then cross-posted them on dozens of similar Websites.

Dartmouth began getting complaints from some scientists who suddenly realized what was going on, but whenever they tried to have "Arky" kicked off their bulletin boards, others would step in and defend him. At the high-end of the argument, people cited his First Amendment rights and, for those outside the United States, the notion that the protocols of science should be broad enough to welcome divergent viewpoints. At the low-end, bemused grad students argued that anyone who was willing to dub himself "The King of All Science" when emailing Nobel

Prize winners with questions about how to pump water up a hose between the Pacific Ocean and the moon using only osmotic pressure, more than gave back in entertainment value what he may have lacked in formal academic credentials.

Those who were hip to what Arky was all about learned to sit back and laugh until the Jolt Cola ran out their nostrils whenever well-known researchers would take the bait and post long, involved responses to the detailed questions he was asking. It was amazing how many scientific heavy hitters, some of them a bit behind the curve because of language differences, would take a break from their multi-million-dollar nuclear accelerators, read Arky's erudite postings, and assume that it was they who were having problems understanding his masterful grip of obscure scientific principles and not the other way around.

From time to time a cult following would develop, and portions of Arky's elaborate discussions would be posted on other Websites like soap opera summaries for those who had missed their shows while on vacation.

Archimedes Plutonium would get entangled with the Zantop case not because of his interest in nuclear physics, but because of some of the other material that he posted when he frequently strayed from his main themes.

Although his "scientific" postings about what he calls Atom Totality Theory run to the thousands of pages and continue to grow daily, Mr. Plutonium has also discussed everything from memories of his childhood, to stock market tips, to observations about religion, to whatever else struck his fancy or was going on in his life.

In a three-year-long series of postings that were remarkable not only for their absolute candor, but also for their inevitable conclusion (which just about everyone but its author could apparently see coming), Archimedes Plutonium posted a complete set of back-and-forth emails written between himself and his supervisors at the Hanover Inn and Dartmouth's personnel office in which he hilariously contested all sorts of aspects of his job as a dishwasher for months on end, both at work and in the courts, until he eventually ended up getting fired in November 1999. Even then it was clear that he was far more worried about when Dartmouth would cut off his employee email account than about his loss of a paycheck.

By January 2001, few remembered Archimedes Plutonium as more than a harmless character who had become an inside joke on parts of the campus. But when the Zantops were found murdered, some began to remember a series of odd coincidences amongst his postings.

What stuck out most was a statement he had posted shortly after his firing from the Hanover Inn.

"Dartmouth is cursed," Plutonium wrote, continuing, "The curse of Dartmouth College is not something I concocted, but rather something I see and observe and report on. God does these things, not me. Dartmouth College will become a science and math desert. A science intellectual desert."

"Dartmouth science professors, instead of helping Archimedes Plutonium, mocked and persecuted AP," the long note on the Internet continued. "Dartmouth laughed at AP for 10 years, now the world will begin to start to laugh and hear bad news about Dartmouth College science and math."

Strictly speaking, Half wasn't exactly a typical scientist, but then again, neither was Arky, and investigators began to wonder if the Geology Department might be close enough for someone they thought wasn't bolted down too tight in the first place.

Also, threaded through the tremendous deluge of musings he had posted on the Net, Archimedes Plutonium said that he had been born in Germany of German parents, and that his father had been a trained gardener. He mentioned hobbies that included bicycling in the countryside, growing fruit and nut trees, picking berries, reading German literature, and collecting rocks and minerals. Certainly nothing there was sinister in its own right, but several people no-

ticed that these were all items that had something of an
overlap with the Zantops, their lifestyle, their interests, and
their careers.

In the days following the murders, Archimedes Plutonium had also written several postings from his new email
accounts about the Zantop case, including one that began,
"I wonder if there were two murder weapons found at the
Zantop residence? If so, that would strongly suggest the
Zantops killed themselves." In his writings he repeatedly
urged detectives to turn away from the homicide investigation and to concentrate instead on the possibility that the
deaths had been a double suicide.

Police and reporters weren't the only ones looking
through the Internet for information about the Zantop killings, and search engines were starting to bring Archimedes
Plutonium's thoughts to the attention of people who were
looking for their own clues. Some of those people began
calling the police.

Looking up Plutonium's email address on the Web, Hanover Detective Eric Bates sent him an email asking that he
call the police station and provide officers with an alibi for
his whereabouts on January 27.

Sitting in his new home, an Airstream trailer out in
South Dakota, Plutonium wasn't about to do any such
thing. He still felt persecuted by Dartmouth, and indeed by
the entire town of Hanover, because of his elaborate firing
two years earlier, and he didn't feel like paying long distance charges just to prove he wasn't a murderer.

When Plutonium didn't respond to Detective Bates' que-
ries, Hanover Police Chief Nick Giaccone joined in with
several emails asking that he call his office.

These too were met with silence, so Giaccone had local
authorities contacted in South Dakota. An officer was sent
out to directly ask Plutonium to get in touch with Hanover
with an alibi.

"I do not like it when police come to my house. It is a
bad image for the neighbors. What do the neighbors think

when police arrive at your home?" Plutonium asked later.

Plutonium still wasn't going to pay for the call, so he sent his phone number to Giaccone via email, and when the chief called him back, Plutonium explained that he had been home in South Dakota happily posting messages throughout the day when the Zantops were killed, and his Internet service provider had the back-up tapes to prove it.

"My Internet posts are like a physical log-in proving my whereabouts," Plutonium said, still upset by his encounter with the investigation months later.

"Dartmouth fired me because of the controversy I stirred with my physics ideas of the Atom Totality Theory," he said. "My science theories created a huge gaggle of haters. And these haters can easily mention my name to the Hanover Police whenever any crime occurs there so as to harass me. This is how the Dartmouth College community railroads people whom they dislike out of town. They conjure up crimes and send the police out after people to get them to move out of town. It's a fun game for haters to play but I see it as a form of police persecution."

The police saw it as an irritating but necessary detour, and turned their attention back to the large pile of leads that were piling up next to the hotline phones that had been set up to draw tips from the public.

chapter 16

Much has been made of criminal "profiling" in recent years because of some notable successes the method has enjoyed. But, as with all good things, by the time it falls into the hands of Hollywood, the fictional presentation of the process has made it look more like a supernatural phenomenon than a helpful set of scientific statistics.

Against that backdrop, investigators were trying to tamp down expectations on Friday, February 9, when it came time to hand out the FBI profiling team's preliminary conclusions to the press.

Shoulder-to-shoulder reporters scanned rapidly down through the handout as copies were passed around the room. Then Kelly Ayotte began to read it for the cameras.

"Information about any suspicious person or unusual vehicle in the area of Trescott Road where the homicides occurred could be extremely important to this investigation. Even if you think that your information is unimportant, or that someone else may have already reported what you know, please contact the Hanover Homicide Task Force Hot Line. Your call may be the one that provides us with the information needed to solve this case," Ayotte read.

"In addition, we are requesting the public's assistance in identifying the offender of these violent crimes. Often, someone in the community will unknowingly associate with the offender of a crime, and may be in a position to observe behavioral changes in that person. They will recognize the changes, and may even question them about it, but will not relate the changes to that person's possible involvement in the homicides," Ayotte continued.

"The Hanover Homicide Task Force has received assistance from the FBI's National Center for the Analysis of Violent Crime. Representatives of that section have been in Hanover consulting with State and local investigators. Based upon their observations, they have determined that person(s) close to the individual responsible for these offenses may have noticed one or more of the following changes and/or scenarios in the offender, since Saturday January 27, 2001," Ayotte said.

Initial enthusiasm among the press corps soon faded to disappointment as she read down the list. Although the profilers had listed a number of things to look for in a possible suspect, they were so broad, they seemed to apply to just about any murder.

1) Unexpectedly leaving the area for a plausible sounding reason (work related, visiting a distant relative or friend, etc.)

2) Unexpectedly arriving in Hanover, NH, area for some plausible sounding reason, perhaps even relating to Dartmouth College or a Hanover area event.

3) Changes in the consumption of alcohol, drugs, or cigarettes.

4) Missing work or other routine engagements, particularly on Saturday January 27 and/or Sunday January 28.

5) An unnatural interest in the status of this investigation, close attention to the media, etc.

6) A noted display of nervousness or irritability.

7) Unexplained injuries/bruises, particularly on the hands or arms.

8) Changes in sleep patterns.

9) Sudden shaving of facial and/or head hair, or the growing of a mustache, beard, etc.

10) No longer operating their vehicle for no plausible reason. This might include suddenly keeping this vehicle in a shed or garage, selling it, giving it away, etc.

"It's important to note the exhibition of one or more of these behavioral changes alone is not indicative of an individual's involvement in these crimes," Ayotte said.

Walking out in the hall as the press conference ended, reporters began to kid Harry Weber, who had been working around the clock on the case as a recent addition to the reporting staff at the Associated Press's Concord bureau, that, according to the profilers, he was the main suspect.

Weber had picked up the "homicide cough" that several reporters had developed from standing out in front of the Zantop residence in an icy breeze during the first several days of the case. He clearly hadn't been getting enough sleep. He hadn't shaved. He had a brand-new car with temporary plates. He had suddenly appeared in Hanover around the time of the murders with a plausible-sounding reason. He had an extreme interest in the case, and was closely watching all the media coverage. To top it off, he was nervous about deadlines and had displayed all kinds of irritation with the pace of the investigation.

"You're it! You're the bogey man," reporter after reporter told a grinning Weber as they shuffled past him and headed out to their cars and satellite trucks.

The brief frivolity masked a deepening sense of frustration that had settled in across the entire investigation. Nothing new seemed to be happening, and in the hallways both detectives and reporters were starting to talk about "other" cases that had gone years before being solved. Some reporters were being pulled out by their editors and assigned to newer, fresher stories, and at the nearby Dartmouth campus, the dull gray winter was settling in hard.

chapter 17

Over the next week the frequency of the press conferences was scaled back to every few days instead of daily, and the investigation continued largely out of public view. But on the morning of Friday, February 16, when most reporters were searching in vain for fresh angles on the Zantop story, the region's largest daily paper sailed in from left field and dropped a bombshell.

The front page headline of *The Boston Globe* read, "Love Affair eyed in N.H. killings: Husband involved with unidentified woman, officials say."

In the article written by reporters Mitchell Zuckoff and Shelley Murphy, the *Globe* quoted unnamed sources close to the investigation who said that detectives were homing in on an extramarital affair involving Half Zantop.

> Hanover, N.H.—Investigators believe the killings of Dartmouth College professors Half and Susanne Zantop were crimes of passion, most likely resulting from an adulterous love affair involving Half Zantop, according to authorities close to the case. The officials said the killings appeared to have been carried out by one person, most likely a man, because "the weapon that was used was heavy, and we don't think a woman would have used it."

The article continued that possible killers might include the enraged husband or boyfriend of whomever Half was seeing. It went on to describe a bloody fight at the crime scene in which Half was quickly disabled and died first, followed closely by a fierce battle with Susanne that raged around the house before she was fatally sliced in the abdomen.

The *Globe* article flabbergasted Hanover, alternately stunning and enraging people who knew the Zantops. It also floored many members of the press corps that had formed around the case. Reporters had quietly (and in a few cases not so quietly) been asking Zantop friends about such background angles just to make sure they weren't missing any obvious possible motives. Now it appeared that they had been caught unprepared after all.

Reporters across town at the *Boston Herald* were just heartsick that they had been scooped on something so major. The same sentiment prevailed in newsrooms across New Hampshire, Massachusetts, and Vermont that had been especially attuned to the case.

In the hours after *The Boston Globe* hit the stands, reporters began pulling up biographical data on every woman they could think of who had been a close friend or associate of Half Zantop. Curricula vitae, résumés, academic conference schedules, and credit reports were all brought in and looked at line by line. Previous interviews with female friends about the Zantops' deaths were re-scrutinized for context clues.

Lists of addresses were made up and photojournalists began quietly shooting surveillance shots of possible "candidates" in the event there was an arrest. But throughout the day, the main message from angry friends to the press was, "No way!" Source after source denied the possibility on the record, on background, and again off the record that Half was having any sort of an affair.

By mid-afternoon the New Hampshire Attorney General's Office took the unusual step of issuing a written reaction to a news story. The statement criticized the *Boston Globe* article and the anonymous sources, and went on to cast doubt on the underlying contention that Half had been having an affair.

Two days later Attorney General Philip McLaughlin

would tackle the question himself at a press conference, and emphatically deny that any affair was being looked into as part of the case, saying, "The *Globe*, from its perspective, was simply relying on what it thought to be reliable information . . . I don't dispute that the *Globe* believed it was accurate, I can only say that which it believed was accurate did not have a shred of support, evidentially speaking, from our perspective."

Hanover Police Chief Nick Giaccone, going one step further, spoke at the same press conference saying, "Suffice it to say that as certain as the Zantops didn't deserve to die, they certainly don't need to have their names smeared in print."

The *Boston Globe* affair article would remain one of the single most memorable features of the case in the minds of the communities that followed it closely. But by the time McLaughlin issued his categorical denunciation of the story, it had already been overshadowed by another series of events.

On Thursday detectives had finally gotten the break they had been looking for. On Friday they had matched it to a pair of suspects. And as the sun came up Saturday morning, those suspects were on the run.

chapter 18

The best clue to the identity of the Zantops' killers had been there all along: the matching plastic knife sheaths on the floor of the study.

From Day One, investigators had realized the potential these items had to be absolutely critical pieces of evidence in the case. The problem was going to be figuring out how to trace them back to their owners.

Unlike individual firearms, knives don't have a unique "ballistic signature," and the wounds inflicted by one brand of knife can appear nearly identical to those which would be created by dozens of other knives. Most states also don't require background checks or impose age limits when knives are bought or sold, and most knives lack the kinds of serial numbers that guns carry which would allow them to be traced back to a particular sale.

Tracking these sheaths was going to require plenty of old-fashioned dogged detective work, and New Hampshire State Police Major Barry Hunter knew he had just the man for the job.

Trooper First Class Charles M. West, 43, had come to the state police in 1984 after having served in the military police in the Air Force and as an officer in Hampton, New Hampshire. In his years on the force, West had earned a reputation as someone who would track leads wherever they led, and Hunter knew this clue was going to require just that sort of tenacious effort.

Both sheaths had already been checked by the New Hampshire State Police Crime Lab for additional evidence, and criminologists had found and lifted two clear fingerprints from one of them. A cross-check of the latent prints from the sheath with the enormous collection of fingerprints on file at the FBI failed to find any matches.

West was paired up with Hanover Police Detective Lieutenant Frank Moran, and together they took a closer look at the sheaths.

Each of the sheaths was made from a single piece of plastic. Molded right into the hard black material on each were the letters "SOG." Each sheath also had a set of two black nylon straps that closed with interlocking black plastic clips. Into the front of one of the sheaths someone had carved a small triangular mark.

"We take what we can get," West said in his only public comments about the case during an interview with *The Boston Globe.* "The sheaths allowed us a specific focus to our investigation. It's a unique item, so we try to find out all we can about them."

West and Moran quickly figured out that "SOG" was the logo of the SOG Specialty Knives & Tools company of Lynnwood, Washington, a well-known manufacturer of knives for sportsmen and the military. The company name was a reference to the famed Studies and Observation Group that had done intelligence work during the Vietnam War.

Of the many kinds of knives that SOG manufactured, only two came with their own unique plastic sheaths. The ones from the Zantops' study matched the model called the SEAL Knife 2000. On Wednesday, January 31, Lieutenant Moran went to a sports store in central New Hampshire and purchased a Seal 2000. He turned it over to New Hampshire State Police Sergeant Mark Mudgett, one of the lead investigators on the case, and Mudgett drove it up to Concord, where New Hampshire Deputy Medical Examiner Dr. Thomas Gilson compared it to the stab wounds that had been documented during the Zantops' autopsies. Dr. Gilson concluded that the injuries to the Zantops could well have been inflicted by a SEAL Knife 2000.

SEAL 2000 are marketed to the world of knife-fanciers as the model that beat out several other combat knives to win a grueling design competition put on by the Navy SEALs.

The real SEALs (whose name comes from an acronym noting their SEa-Air-and-Land attack capabilities) are an American special forces unit that constitutes a small but impressive asset the Navy can roll out in wartime. Their best-known alumnus is probably Minnesota Governor Jesse Ventura. Jesse aside, in the largely peaceful decades following the Vietnam War, thanks mostly to a few good books and several really bad movies, the SEALs blossomed from the ranks of obscure military trivia onto center stage in the imaginations of commando-wannabes everywhere.

From practically unknown to practically a cottage industry in a few short years, the SEALs seem to occupy a part of the sub-cultural imagination that also likes to delve into ninjas, poisonous snakes, and movies featuring beautiful Russian women who have been trained to operate complex nuclear weapons and wear short skirts and high heels while they do so.

It's possible to buy SEAL t-shirts, SEAL workout videos, SEAL sniper videos, SEAL wet suits, SEAL swimsuits, SEAL meals, and probably even SEAL fuzzy bathroom slippers if you look hard enough. Many of these party favors marketed with SEAL emblems and logos are of dubious military use, but the SOG SEAL Knife 2000 is actually a serious piece of equipment with a real connection to the Navy's special forces organization.

In the 1990s the Navy quartermasters who order non-military standard equipment for the SEALs invited knife manufacturers to submit candidates for an "official" SEAL knife. Although a government contract wasn't guaranteed, it was understood that the winning knife would be the one the SEALs would use as their standard issue within the organization.

The SEALs tested how much pressure was needed to

break off the tips of the various candidate knives. They soaked them in gasoline and salt water for weeks at a time looking for corrosion. They burned the knives with acetylene torches and chopped, pried, hammered, and cut all kinds of different ropes, wires, and cables with them. They looked at them in sunlight and again in moonlight for any telltale reflections that could give away a commando's position, and they listened to how much noise each knife made when scraped over different surfaces. In the end, the modified Bowie knife submitted by SOG was declared the winner and it became the SEAL Knife 2000.

The SOG SEAL 2000 is not your grandmother's butter knife.

For starters, each one is heavy, nearly 13 ounces, and just over a foot long—12.25 inches from tip to pommel.

Fully seven inches of that is the blade. It's made of razor-sharp Japanese 440A stainless steel with one-and-a-half inches of serrated teeth along the bottom, all of which has been powder-coated in a dark gray scratch-resistant finish. The blade is 2.75 inches at its widest point and features a full tang which is encased in a hard molded black handle made from a fiberglass-reinforced plastic material called Zytel. The handle is scored with a small diamond checker pattern across it to allow for a firm grip. It's not just a tool, it's a deadly weapon designed to stab people to death.

As one breathless ad on the Internet put it, "The SEAL-Knife-2000 is perhaps the most anxiously awaited and dramatically new fixed blade to come along in years, and it's now available for the civilian market without any changes. You can be assured on this amazing knife that the SEALs have done their homework . . . so you don't have to."

West and Moran *did* have a lot of homework left to do. They immediately contacted Vicky Karshna, SOG's Assistant Marketing Director, with a subpoena asking for records from the sales department. By Friday, February 2, they had a list, state by state, of all authorized SOG dealers in the country. The list was huge, stretching into the hundreds, and there was always the possibility that one of the listed retailers or distributors had sold the knives on one of their Websites, or that the knives used in the homicide had been bought second-hand through a private sale or some other forum.

Despite the range of other options, the detectives' hope was that they could find someone in the region who had recently purchased two identical knives over the counter. If not, West was going to have to take a crash course in how to work the Internet.

Day after day, the pair made their way down the list, calling and visiting knife dealers and sporting goods stores through New Hampshire, Vermont, and Maine. Nothing turned up, and the fear began to grow that perhaps someone had purchased the knives in a manner that didn't leave a paper trail.

"You have cash sales, non-traceable transactions, and you just have to deal with them," West told *The Boston Globe*. "You have to keep a good mind frame on these type of cases, because you could easily get distracted," he added.

On the plus side, even though the SOG SEAL Knife 2000 had been manufactured for several years, the hard black sheaths, made out of a plastic called Kydex, were relatively new. SOG had only begun shipping Kydex sheaths with these knives early in the year 2000.

Hearing again and again from retailers that lots of knives were now being sold on-line, West bit the bullet and started learning to surf the Net. He had only started to experiment with the Web himself at the first of the year and now, just over a month later, he was having to use it to try to solve one of the state's most baffling crimes.

Still, nothing turned up, but as the FBI joined the investigation, they sent agents in Washington state on another visit to SOG's headquarters with subpoenas, asking employees there to help them narrow the list of distributors to just those who had sold SEAL 2000s with the new Kydex sheaths.

That new and improved list was handed over to the FBI and forwarded to the New Hampshire detectives on Monday, February 12. It still left about 5,000 knife sales to be scrutinized nationwide, but by this point, West and Moran had already investigated a substantial number of those. They had also noticed that one of the listed dealers, Fox Firearms of Scituate, Massachusetts, was auctioning a couple of hundred knives at a time, including SEAL 2000s, on the popular Internet auction site eBay.

Two days later, as he was culling his way down through the list, West called James Fox, who owns Fox Firearms, and asked him for a list of all the new SOG SEAL 2000s he had sold.

Fox told West that his last wholesale purchase of SEAL 2000s from SOG had been for 120 of the knives, and he only had about forty left. He forwarded West a list of all his recent sales of that particular knife.

When Trooper West looked at Fox's list, one of those sales immediately jumped out at him.

Of the 84 sales that Fox had recently completed, there was just one order for two identical SOG SEAL 2000s. It had been placed on New Year's Day, January 1, 2001, less than a month before the murders.

The purchaser was listed as Jim Parker of Chelsea, Vermont—a town that sits only twenty-three miles northwest as the crow flies from where the Zantops had been killed.

Examining that particular sale closely, West found that Parker, using the email address jimibruce@hotmail.com, had arranged the purchase of the knives in a series of emails on January 1 and January 2. Although the knives typically list for around $130 apiece, Parker had spent the first two days of the new year negotiating a price of $180 for the double purchase.

Fox's records showed that Parker had mailed him a money order for the purchase on Sunday, January 7, requesting two-day delivery to "James Parker, 10 Bradshaw Crossroad, Chelsea, VT 05038." On January 11, Parker had emailed Fox again, requesting confirmation that the knives had been shipped.

It was now late afternoon on Valentine's Day, February 14, but Trooper West and several other detectives from the Hanover Homicide Task Force began making plans to go take a closer look at Chelsea, Vermont, the next day.

chapter 19

At 6:30 P.M. on Thursday, February 15, unmarked police cruisers began pulling up in front of a two-story reddish-brown saltbox-style house with rose-colored trim that had been lovingly constructed by its owner, a local home builder named John Parker, on the Bradshaw Crossroad, way up in the steep hills towering over the western side of the village of Chelsea.

New Hampshire State Police Sergeant Robert Bruno, Trooper Russell Hubbard, and Vermont State Police Sergeant Tim Page walked over the snow-shrouded walkway and rang the doorbell. John Parker and his son Jimmy, a tall, thin 16-year-old, were home at the time, and when the detectives identified themselves as investigators from the Zantop homicide, John Parker invited them in.

Sitting down around the family's dining room table with a now noticeably nervous Jimmy Parker and his father, the detectives explained that they were checking all the recent purchases of a particular model of SOG knife, and they wanted to know about the pair that "Jim" Parker had purchased earlier that month.

Jimmy told the detectives that he had indeed ordered two of the knives, but added that he hadn't told his parents because he knew that his mother would be upset by such a purchase. The teen couldn't recall the precise date he had ordered the knives or when they were received, but he remembered getting them by Priority Mail at his house.

Once he received them, Jimmy told detectives, he took the knives over to the house of his friend Robert Tulloch in the center of Chelsea village, and there they both opened the boxes and discarded the packaging and shipping materials.

Parker said the knives came with sheaths made out of a material called "Kindex," but he said that neither he nor Tulloch had added any straps or clasps, and he said they did not make any markings on their sheaths either.

Where then were the knives? detectives wondered.

They were gone, according to Parker. He and Tulloch had taken them into the woods a couple of times and used them to cut branches for a fort, but found the knives to be too heavy. The pair decided to sell them, Parker explained, and on the weekend of either January 20 or January 27, he had driven with Rob Tulloch to Burlington, the only city of any real size in Vermont, and gone into an Army/Navy store with the intention of trying to interest the store clerk in purchasing the knives.

As he walked up to the clerk and displayed the knives, Parker said, another customer in the store, a white male with brown hair and a five o'clock shadow, took him aside and looked the knives over. After a careful inspection, the stranger offered to buy both knives for $60 apiece, and Parker said he sold them on the spot.

After listening to Parker's story for just over an hour, detectives asked if he and his father would be willing to come down to the Orange County Sheriff's Office in the center of Chelsea, where Jimmy could voluntarily provide a set of fingerprints for elimination purposes. With his father seated beside him, Parker had little choice but to agree, and the pair drove behind the detectives to the sheriff's house-like brick office.

At the sheriff's office, Sergeant West, who had put so much time in tracking the knives, was waiting. As Jimmy Parker was busy signing written consent forms, going through the fingerprinting process, and preparing another written statement about the purchase with Sergeant West, the other officers had left and gone across the town common to pay a visit to Robert Tulloch.

At 8:06 P.M., Sergeants Bruno and Page, and Trooper Hubbard, stepped onto the ornate front porch of the large yellow antique house at 313 Main Street in the heart of Chelsea's village center.

Robert Tulloch, 17, was home with his parents, Michael and Diane Tulloch, when the detectives arrived and identified themselves as investigators from the Zantop case. The detectives made a mental note that Tulloch also was about six feet tall and thin, and the three officers sat down with the Tullochs in the living room to listen as Robert Tulloch voluntarily told them his story.

It was the same account the detectives had just received from Jimmy Parker. Tulloch said that his friend had ordered the knives, but that he couldn't recall specific dates of order and delivery. He said the knives had been used to cut branches in the woods, but proved too heavy. Tulloch claimed that Jimmy had sold the knives to someone he had chanced upon at an Army/Navy store on a day when the pair had gone to Burlington to do some simulated rock climbing at an indoor facility.

Tulloch said that the pair had driven to Burlington in Parker's car that day, but Parker had been the only one to go into the Army/Navy store to make the knife sale.

The detectives also asked Robert Tulloch about a knee injury he had sustained the weekend of the murders. Tulloch told them that he had a small but deep cut just above his right knee that he had received when he walked down an embankment to go to the bathroom in the woods. He said that he had slid into an old metal maple syrup tap spigot that was still stuck in a tree. Tulloch said that in hindsight, he probably should have had stitches, but didn't. His mother Diane, who worked as a visiting nurse based at the nearby Gifford Medical Center hospital in Randolph, Vermont, told the detectives that she had looked at it and thought it was okay.

While this was going on, Jimmy Parker had signed a written consent form along with his father, and was going through the fingerprinting process as detectives watched closely. By 8:30 P.M., Jimmy was giving another written statement about his purchase of the knives to Sergeant West, followed by another interview, again with his father present, this time on audiotape, explaining once again how he had come to purchase the knives. Each of Parker's interviews was consistent with the previous one, and in the taped interview he added that he had kept the two knives in his bedroom bureau prior to selling them to the stranger.

In the meantime, the Tullochs gave the officers permission to fingerprint Robert. The family hopped in their car and followed the investigators on the short drive around the snow-covered common to the sheriff's office.

At 8:50 P.M., after the prints had been taken, Trooper Hubbard asked Tulloch's parents if they would have any objection if he went back to the house and took some of Robert's footwear for comparison purposes. They said they didn't, and once they got back home, father, mother, and son all signed a Consent to Search and Seizure, and Robert Tulloch brought two sets of footwear into the kitchen. Michael Tulloch stated that the Vasque hiking boots were his son's only pair of winter boots, and Trooper Hubbard and Sergeant Bruno took them and left the home a short time later.

The Parkers didn't leave the sheriff's office until 10 P.M., by which time Sergeant West had also had an opportunity to sit down and talk one-on-one with John Parker about the weekend of January 27–28. The elder Parker first recalled that his son spent that Saturday and that Saturday night with Robert Tulloch. However, after Sergeant West asked Jimmy about his whereabouts that day and Jimmy couldn't recall, his father indicated that he too could not be certain where Jimmy had been on the day of the murders.

Sergeant West followed the Parkers back to their house and received permission to conduct a similar search of Jimmy Parker's footwear; however, he didn't find any

Dartmouth Hall sits in the middle of the college's campus. Susanne Zantop's offices were located in this building. At left can be seen Rollins Chapel, where a memorial service was held for the murdered professors. *(Eric Francis)*

Flowers placed outside the office of Susanne Zantop. *(Eric Francis)*

THE DAY
AFTER THE MURDERS: The Major Crimes Unit van backs into the Zantops' driveway.

An officer videotapes Roxana Verona's car in front of the Zantops' house.

Troopers take away evidence. Behind them can be seen the stone wall that runs along most of the Zantop property.
(All photos by Eric Francis)

The Zantop house, as seen from Trescott Road. The window at left looks into the study. *(Eric Francis)*

The Chelsea Public School, which both Robert Tulloch and Jimmy Parker attended *(Eric Francis)*

Jimmy Parker, kneeling at left, and Robert Tulloch, standing at right, prepare the boat they built for the Annual Chelsea Town Raft Race. *(Photo by Jeb Wallace-Brodeur)*

Hood House and Chelsea Mills, Robert Tulloch's home in Chelsea. *(Eric Francis)*

Sturbridge Isle truck stop in Massachusetts, where Jimmy Parker and Robert Tulloch ditched their car and started hitching rides across the country with various truckers. *(Eric Francis)*

Christiana Usenza, who had been Robert Tulloch's girlfriend, speaks with the press. The New Hampshire Attorney General had told Christiana she was not a target of the criminal investigation. *(Eric Francis)*

Col. Gary Sloper and New Hampshire officials unveil to the press photos of the suspects and the silver Audi they left at Sturbridge Isle. *(Eric Francis)*

Jimmy Parker is led from the FBI jet and turned over to the State of New Hampshire. *(Eric Francis)*

New Hampshire Assistant Attorney General Kelly Ayotte. Behind her is Hanover Police Chief Nicholas Giaccone. *(Eric Francis)*

New Hampshire Attorney General Philip McLaughlin briefs the press. At far left stands Hanover Police Chief Nicholas Giaccone. New Hampshire State Police Major Barry Hunter stands between them. *(Eric Francis)*

Dartmouth President James Wright speaks about the murders. *(Eric Francis)*

shoes matching the descriptions investigators were looking for, and left the house empty-handed.

It was now pushing towards midnight Thursday, and as Sergeant Bruno drove Robert Tulloch's hiking boots and both boys' fingerprint cards back to the New Hampshire State Police Forensic Laboratory a couple of hours away, the rest of the investigation was calling it a night. In the morning they would all gather again in the Hanover war room and think over what the two boys and their families had said in their separate interviews, and compare the details of their stories. More importantly, criminologists in Concord would get a chance first thing Friday morning to compare the fingerprints and footwear with the evidence found at the Zantop crime scene.

Sergeant Bruno knew that it would only take a few minutes to tell whether or not the fingerprints and the boot prints were in any way connected to the murders, and thus rule the boys out . . . or perhaps rule them in. As Bruno and the other detectives drove away, that same realization was dawning on two very alarmed teenagers.

chapter 20

After the awkward appearance of the police at his doorstep, which had suddenly made it necessary to tell his parents that he had been the clandestine co-purchaser of a knife scary enough to land him in the middle of a homicide investigation, Robert Tulloch wasted no time getting on the phone and calling friends.

He made several calls to 19-year-old Christiana Usenza, his sometime girlfriend with whom he had been friends since the pair played soccer together at age eleven. Christiana had changed schools her senior year, and had actually graduated in mid-January, but she still considered Tulloch her boyfriend.

"He's been my friend since middle school, a very close friend of mine. He was my boyfriend at times through my last years of high school," recalled Christiana.

After the police left with his boots, Rob called Christiana twice and left messages on her answering machine asking her to call him and saying it was urgent.

When Christiana returned home that evening, sometime after 10 P.M., from her job at a grocery store in Montpelier, she skipped her answering machine messages altogether and simply called Robert to see how his day had been. She found him in a swivet.

Rob told Christiana that he had just been questioned by police in connection with the Zantop homicide.

"What? That's really horrible!" Christiana replied, adding, "Why you?"

Rob explained that there was a connection, because he had purchased a hunting knife over the Internet, and he knew that that was how police could have linked him to the investigation. He told her that he and Jimmy had bought the knife for the extended trip out West they had been planning for some time.

"I was very, very shocked," Christiana said.

Rob had been getting over a fever earlier in the week and was still a bit sick, and wanted to get off the phone.

"He seemed very shocked. It was a very brief conversation," Christiana recalled.

The two friends said goodnight and Christiana went to bed thinking that she would discuss the matter further with Rob the next day.

Officials may not have realized how close they were to their prime suspects, but it seemed as though the boys may have, and at 3 A.M., Jimmy left his home in the silver Audi that had once been his older sister's, and headed down the hills for Robert Tulloch's house.

Hearing his son leave in the middle of the night, John Parker got up, and a short time later drove out looking for him. He checked around the village and drove by Tulloch's house, but he couldn't see Jimmy's car. Concerned, John drove home, where he and Joan waited up much of the night for Jimmy to return. It had been a disturbing evening, but the police had not given the Parkers any reason to believe that their son was a suspect in a double homicide. In fact, it was quite the opposite: The police had looked around Jimmy's room and left empty-handed, they hadn't called him a suspect or even a witness, and they had assured the family that they were just eliminating possibilities from a long list of people who had purchased the same type of knife over the Internet.

As the sun came up and daylight suffused the house high above Chelsea village, John Parker spotted a handwritten note from his son that he had overlooked in the dark. It said that Jimmy had gone to visit Rob. "Don't call the cops. I'll be back in the morning," Jimmy wrote.

Confused, John Parker settled in at his home to wait for his son.

As the business day started Friday, technicians at the State Forensic Lab in New Hampshire unpacked the Vasque boots seized from Robert Tulloch. Criminalist Morris Boudreau checked the boot against the clearest of the bloody partial footwear impressions that were found on the Zantops' living room floor, adjacent to the entry to the study. The bloodstain pattern matched Tulloch's left boot. Laboratory Director Timothy Piper carefully verified the match, and picked up the phone.

At the same time technicians were poring over Robert Tulloch's boots, concern and conscience were twisting John Parker. He started placing calls around the town trying to find out where Jimmy might have gone. He called the Tulloch family and learned that they hadn't seen either boy that morning, and had assumed that Rob was with Jimmy somewhere. John Parker waited until 11 A.M., and then he picked up the phone again and dialed police.

Word from the criminologists at the lab that the teens from Chelsea were suddenly starting to match the evidence at the Etna crime scene hit the Hanover Homicide Task Force investigators at almost the same moment that they learned from John Parker that the boys weren't home and hadn't been seen for eight hours.

While most of the Upper Valley was spending that Friday morning trying to decide what to think about the *Boston Globe* headline saying that Half's infidelity was the motive for the killings, investigators were scrambling behind the scenes to sort out how to deal with the fact that they had found, and then lost, their prime suspects in less than twelve hours' time.

Chelsea residents, who normally by mid-February are desperately hoping that something out of the ordinary will break up the monotony of winter, began to notice a lot of unusual activity around the town's twin commons as Friday progressed. In a town with only one main road and all municipal offices ringed around the unique "twin commons," residents quickly picked up on the heavy police presence that was pouring into the community.

Marked and unmarked police cars began to pile up outside the offices of Orange County Sheriff Dennis McClure as New Hampshire State Police and Hanover detectives tried to learn what they could about the two boys. Soon the Vermont State Police started arriving in force to help with the investigation, and residents also spotted cars out on the hunt for the pair that was already quietly under way around the back roads of the town.

Detectives began talking to teachers and friends of the two teens from the Chelsea high school, and the more they learned about them, the more two things in particular stood out:

Detectives were told that on the Monday morning after the Zantop murders, the boys had been back in school, but Robert Tulloch had been sporting a large knee bandage and walking with a painful limp from an injury for which he had a particularly implausible explanation. Nobody walks around the woods of Vermont building forts in mid-February, especially without snowshoes, and the odds of sliding into an old but sharp syrup tap, considering that brand-new ones aren't particularly sharp in the first place, just didn't ring true. However, detectives knew that, at a minimum, Susanne Zantop had fought and fought hard, and, as the FBI had pointed out, it was quite possible that her attackers would have some injury to show for it.

The second thing that struck detectives as odd was that on Wednesday, January 31, less than four days after the murders, the boys had amazed their friends by suddenly taking off together on an inexplicable cross-country trip that seemed to brew up out of nowhere, and which turned out to have been miserably planned, if at all.

No one seemed to have seen the boys on the Saturday or Sunday in question, but the two had been in school on

Monday, seemingly normal except for Tulloch's pronounced limp.

On Monday and Tuesday, both Tulloch and Parker had spent some time at the homes of their classmates Gaelen McKee and Zach Courts, but those boys' parents couldn't recall either Rob or Jimmy saying or doing anything unusual while they were visiting.

During those few days, Parker suddenly put his snowboard up for sale. After he collected $200, a lot less than it was worth, Jimmy and Rob made plans to head out across the country via bus.

Rob told Christiana Usenza that he and Jimmy were bored in Chelsea, especially in the wake of their recent winter break, and that they felt it was time to go and see the rest of the country.

Most of the pair's friends weren't told of their plans to depart, but Rob discussed some of the details with Christiana, including the fact that neither boy's parents knew that they were on the brink of leaving. He also told her that he had made up the syrup tap story and said that he had really cut his leg when he had accidentally dropped a hunting knife on it. Rob also told Christiana that the impending trip was more than a short lark, it was good-bye to Chelsea. Rob wasn't sure where the pair were going to go but he was sure they were going to stay out of Vermont for quite a while.

"They told me that they were going on a trip that they had been planning for a long time. They didn't know exactly where they were going to go. But they were hoping to start lives somewhere out West," Christiana recalled. "I knew that their parents didn't know," she admitted. She assumed they had bought tickets to Colorado, since they had talked often in the past of wanting to travel out there and go rock climbing.

Finally, as they were getting ready to leave, Rob stopped in at the grocery store in Montpelier when Christiana was working to give her his teddy bear. The gesture struck Christiana as sweet.

On the morning of Wednesday, January 31, the boys took Jimmy's silver Audi and drove the thirty-five miles down from Chelsea to the Vermont Transit bus terminal in White River Junction, Vermont—a tiny transportation hub at the geographic center of Vermont and New Hampshire— looking to buy bus tickets to California.

The ticket agents at the bus station are used to keeping an eye open for runaways, felons, and escapees from the mental wards at the nearby Veterans Administration hospital, but as a pair, Tulloch and Parker didn't raise any particular concerns. The one odd thing that stood out in hindsight was that they had initially wanted to go to a non-existent destination.

"The only thing that was unusual was that they just didn't know where they wanted to go," recalled ticket agent Brenda Johnson. "They acted perfectly normal. They knew they wanted to go somewhere, but they didn't know for sure just where."

Tulloch and Parker first asked for two one-way tickets to Syracuse, California.

"I thought that's in New York," Johnson replied.

No, they said, it's in California.

"Do you mean Santa Cruz?" Johnson asked.

Again, the teens insisted they wanted Syracuse, California. Johnson shrugged and typed it into her Greyhound bus lines ticketing computer, but nothing by that name came up.

In any event, Johnson informed the boys, one-way tickets from Vermont to anywhere in California would run them $159 apiece. They didn't have that much money.

Where could they go that was warm for about twenty dollars less? they wondered.

Johnson handed over an atlas and traced out a rough arc across the Midwest with her fingertip. Tulloch and Parker sat quietly on a nearby row of chairs before making their decision and coming back up to the counter.

They wanted to go to Amarillo, Texas. One-way. Departing that afternoon.

At 11:10 A.M., they each paid $139 for tickets on the bus that left White River Junction at 1:50 P.M. headed down Interstate 91 towards New York City and points south.

Parker filled out a two-week registration card allowing him to leave his silver Audi in the bus station parking lot through February 13, but said they didn't expect it to be there nearly that long. He used his real name on the form. "To my knowledge, someone was supposed to come and pick up the car later that day. Whether or not they did, I don't know," Johnson said.

Each boy then checked a backpack as luggage and settled down to wait the nearly three hours until the bus departed.

"They were just dressed casually. They paid cash for the tickets," Johnson said, adding, "They didn't bring attention to themselves. They were quiet."

The bus ride was a long one, and after the 45-minute layover in New York City, where the pair changed from the white-and-green Vermont Transit bus to a Greyhound headed to St. Louis, there was little to do on the 33-hour trip but stare out the windows or try to sleep. Both were becoming difficult for Tulloch as the untreated wound to his leg became more and more painful.

Chelsea's public school system has built so much slack into their graduation requirements that many students can quickly accumulate enough credits during their first three years of high school to essentially take a year-long vacation during their senior year. Tulloch had already done that, and in fact, he hadn't even bothered to formally enroll for the fall 2001 term. Parker was on the same track; however, even by Chelsea's loose standards, the notion that a senior like Tulloch, let alone a junior like Parker, could just waltz off in the middle of the school year was a new one. Tulloch and Parker were missed, and classmates began to circulate vague tales that they had taken off on a lark to Colorado to go rock climbing or skiing. Friends were a bit amazed, but they wrote it off as "senioritis" on Tulloch's part.

Late Thursday evening, on February 1, the boys reached St. Louis, and by now, the reality of Tulloch's leg injury, their fatigue, their utter lack of cash, and homesickness were beginning to mount.

Jimmy Parker picked up the phone and called his mother back in Vermont. Initially he just tried to tell her that he was okay, but he couldn't say where he was. The Tullochs and the Parkers, used to some absences and pretty loose schedules—but not like this—had already noticed that the boys were gone from town. Joan Parker would later tell friends that she was on the brink of getting the police involved and reporting Jimmy as a missing person when he called. The Parkers laid down the law and demanded to know what was going on. Jimmy caved and said that he and Robert were in St. Louis, were out of money, and would like to get Rob's leg some medical attention as soon as possible.

Infuriated at this seemingly pointless stunt, the Parkers started calling airlines and booked the pair a flight back to Manchester, New Hampshire, via Chicago. Early on Friday morning, the boys boarded a plane in St. Louis and started heading home.

During the layover at O'Hare International Airport in Chicago, the boys called Christiana Usenza and asked her to come get them when they landed in New Hampshire.

"They called me from Chicago saying, 'We're coming home. We decided that this isn't the right time to be doing this [because] we really don't have enough money,'" Christiana said, adding with a nervous laugh, "They said, 'We saw America, we didn't like it, and we want to come home.'"

Rob told Christiana that the cut to his leg was getting infected and he didn't have enough money with him to have it treated in St. Louis. She met them at the airport and drove them back up Interstate 89 to Vermont, where they stopped at the Vermont Transit bus station in White River Junction and picked up Jimmy's car.

Parker's parents were furious with Jimmy and his explanations for what had just happened, and, according to friends, they "grounded him for life." His car was taken away; he was not to watch television or use his computer. As part of his punishment, he was flat-out forbidden to visit Rob for at least a month. But a few days later, both boys reappeared at the bus station in White River Junction looking for a refund on the unused portions of their tickets.

"It was two, three, or maybe four days later—whatever," recalled Johnson. "Basically they said that because of some weather delays and the schedule change that resulted, they decided not to complete the trip. They said they did make it to St. Louis and that was it."

Johnson refunded them each $20 for the unused segment of their trip to Amarillo and thought little of it until their pictures began appearing on CNN and in the local newspapers two weeks later. "They were very clean-cut–looking kids. It's just hard to believe it," Johnson said.

Investigators working through the day on Friday, February 16, began to piece together all the information surrounding the boys' previous trip to St. Louis. They were becoming increasingly convinced that they were looking at suspects who had already made one serious attempt to flee the jurisdiction, and were probably doing something quite similar at that very moment.

After fingerprints from the boys had been compared to those lifted from the knife sheaths and a chair in the Zantops' study, New Hampshire investigators were convinced that they wanted Robert Tulloch and James Parker brought in for questioning in connection with the homicides.

Around 1 P.M. on Friday, the decision was made to issue a "B-O-L," or "be on the lookout," notice to police officers throughout Vermont and New Hampshire, but because of the large media presence that was still in the region covering the case, it was decided not to put it out over police radios. Instead, a series of alerts were issued to police across the Twin States ordering officers to call or stop by their stations for information. When they did, they were provided with descriptions of Tulloch and Parker and the Audi, and told that the boys were considered armed and dangerous and were likely to be traveling along back roads, possibly headed for Windsor, Vermont.

Reporters may not have had the details, but they certainly knew something was up when they heard the unusually wide-ranging call-the-station broadcasts and listened to the sudden increase in tempo among the police units in the region. Even more intriguing, those units seemed to be spending a lot of time looking for a particular vehicle on the back roads of Orange and Windsor Counties in Vermont.

Vermont State Police began to worry about what Tulloch and Parker might do if they realized that there was a search under way, and they became concerned about the boys' ready access to the Chelsea Public School.

The barn-like school building beside the South Common houses all the town's 272 students, from Kindergarten through the twelfth grade, and averages only about sixteen students per class, although the high school section of the building jumps to between thirty and forty students per grade because of tuition students from nearby small towns.

At 1:30 P.M., the Vermont State Police called Chelsea Principal Patricia Davenport and asked her whether Tulloch and Parker were in school. When Davenport told the trooper that the boys had been reported absent, she was informed that they were both involved "in a dangerous situation," and that she should call police immediately if they came to school or to the gym after classes were over.

Davenport walked around the school building making sure all the doors, several of which have safety bars, were locked, and then asked a couple of teachers to stay out in the hall and the main lobby area and keep the other students in their classrooms.

School officials called police and the sheriff's office trying to get information, but none was forthcoming, and teachers were never told that the teens were suspected of a violent crime. Students noticed a police car stationed outside, and saw detectives checking out their buses, but the day ended without the Chelsea Public School having any idea what was going on.

By Friday evening, police in two states had all of their paperwork together and the first set of warrants charging Robert Tulloch with two counts of first-degree murder were issued. Tulloch, being 17, was easier to prepare papers for, since he was an adult under New Hampshire law. Parker, just three months shy of his seventeenth birthday, was still considered a juvenile, and was going to require more effort from prosecutors.

Late Friday night, warrants were issued for Robert W. Tulloch of 313 Main Street in Chelsea on two counts of first-degree murder. Police noted that he might be driving a silver-colored 1987 Audi 5000 four-door sedan bearing Vermont registration CDG690. The warrant mentioned that Tulloch might also be in the company of a 16-year-old male.

At 10:30 P.M., a Vermont State Police mobile crime lab truck pulled up to the bright yellow home with the sweeping front porch and its pair of Adirondack chairs. Detectives began to search Robert Tulloch's room while his family was forced to spend the night in an area hotel.

All night long, neighbors could see detectives' flashlights shining back and forth behind a large American flag that hung in the window of Robert's bedroom on the second floor of the house. Police cars would remain on the scene well into Saturday night as evidence was gathered.

Late Friday evening, the news that Tulloch and another teen from Chelsea were being sought for killing the Zantops was faxed to the media, and as the sun came up Saturday, a nationwide manhunt was on.

chapter 21

Police were concerned that two desperate teenagers on the run with little money might do something drastic and harm someone else, given that the police thought they had already killed two unarmed people in their own home in broad daylight.

To put all the necessary resources into capturing the pair, New Hampshire detectives first had to clear a technical hurdle created by Parker's age. The three months he was short of his seventeenth birthday made him a juvenile under New Hampshire law. Police were free to broadcast Tulloch's picture and information, but authorities legally could only refer to Parker as "an accompanying juvenile."

Over the noon hour on Saturday, February 17, New Hampshire Attorney General Philip McLaughlin put forward a legal petition asking that Parker be treated as an adult "for purposes of apprehension." A judge in Littleton signed the order.

Later Saturday afternoon, Kelly Ayotte stepped back up to the microphones in Hanover and read the boys' information out to the phalanx of television cameras and reporters present.

Each of the arrest warrants charged both of the boys with two counts apiece of first-degree murder "acting in concert with and aided by" the other.

Because it appeared that the suspects had crossed the state line from Vermont into New Hampshire to commit the crime, and since it was likely that they had done something similar to avoid being captured on Friday, the FBI stepped in and issued a set of UFAPs, or unlawful flight to avoid prosecution warrants, that gave federal agents the go-ahead to commit their resources across the country to track-ing and catching the teens. Within minutes, the boys' pictures were posted on the FBI's Website.

Ayotte's press conference naming the suspects was the first time that the press learned on the record that both of the Zantops had been stabbed repeatedly in the head and chest, and that officials believed the boys brought the knives with them to the Zantops' home.

With the suspects' pictures now posted next to the po-dium where officials had given so many cryptic press con-ferences before, and a major chapter in the case clearly behind him, Hanover Police Chief Nick Giaccone stepped up to the mikes. "I really want to thank the worker bees, the detectives from the New Hampshire State Police, and the detectives of my department, and my officers; they are the ones that, when given the task, have really, really made this happen," Giaccone said, adding, "The case is far from over, these individuals have not been apprehended yet, and they may very well be apprehended in another jurisdiction where those worker bees will be helping us bring these individuals to justice."

Back in Chelsea, two mobile crime scene trucks from Vermont and New Hampshire, accompanied by numerous cruisers, made their way up the snow-covered dirt roads of West Hill to the Parker residence. It was the Parker family's turn to move out to a local hotel as detectives executed search warrants on the residence and especially Jimmy's bedroom. Two of the family's other cars, a green 1996 Subaru station wagon and a newer small blue Honda, both of which Jimmy had driven in recent weeks, were also im-pounded and put on flatbed tow trucks from Ward's Garage for the ride to the Vermont State Police Headquarters in Middlesex, where they would be minutely searched.

Although the details wouldn't be released to the press for weeks, the detectives who were continuing to search both the Parker and Tulloch residences had begun finding critical pieces of evidence that appeared to be linked to the Zantop killings.

Detectives already knew that the fingerprints on one of the knife sheaths had been matched to Jimmy Parker. Now, as they searched his cluttered bedroom on the first floor of the Bradshaw Crossroad residence, they seized the clothes and bed linens from his room, and pulled his other dirty laundry from the laundry room.

Police also seized two computers and seventy diskettes from the Parker residence, along with an answering machine, a Rolodex, various printouts, receipts, handwritten notes, and a list of phone numbers. A honing stone with honing oil for knife sharpening were also taken, as were Jimmy's ID cards for the Killington and Stowe ski resorts. Police also took a picture that they cryptically said "involved a chainsaw."

Parker's mother's green Subaru was in the driveway when Sergeant Susan Foiri and Sergeant Russell Conte of the New Hampshire State Police's Major Crimes Unit took a good look at it from the outside using a flashlight. Conte could see a light red stain in the center of the floor mat on the front passenger side of the car. Conte thought it looked like a bloodstain, and, aware that the bloody boot prints had matched Tulloch's boots, and that Parker usually drove, Conte ordered the car seized and the carpet tested.

Down at the Tulloch residence on Main Street in Chelsea, Vermont State Police Detective Ray Keefe and the other Vermont and New Hampshire officers searching Robert Tulloch's second-floor bedroom had hit the jackpot. In a cardboard Florida citrus box, two SOG SEAL 2000 knives had been hidden under a layer of magazines. Both knives had been placed in homemade sheaths constructed from foam rubber wrapped in duct tape.

In the coming weeks of forensic testing at the crime lab, detectives and criminologists would discover blood on both knives, on Robert's left boot, and on the passenger-side carpet in Joan Parker's Subaru. In court documents, the detectives asserted that the DNA testing of the blood on one knife matched Susanne Zantop while the blood on the other knife matched both Susanne and Half.

The blood on Robert's boot was a mix of blood from Susanne and an unknown male. Police didn't yet have a sample of Rob's blood, but they expected it would match that of the unknown male when they finally had a chance to test it. Susanne's blood was also found on the car's carpet.

Sitting on the chair in Rob's bedroom was a black spiral-bound notebook which appeared to contain notes regarding the surveillance of a building. A gray pullover sweater, a gray suitcoat, gray vest, gray suit pants, and two white socks were draped over the same chair along with one red sock, a pair of tan pants, a pair of dark blue underwear, and a white T-shirt.

Nearby was a blue waste basket with a Band-Aid and an Ace wrap bandage sitting on the floor in front of it. Emptying the waste basket, detectives found a bloody wad of tissue paper, two white ankle socks (one had an unidentified hair attached to it and the other was stained, possibly with blood), two additional pieces of a white sock with stains, three plastic bags (two with cardboard inserts, the third with a "warning label" on it), a piece of carbon paper, and a piece of paper with writing that mentioned "UPS."

From Robert's bookcase, police seized a roll of self-adhesive Ace wrap, a copy of a book about Adolf Hitler entitled *Der Fuehrer*, a folder with papers containing personal writings, a blue notebook, and a deflated football.

Another black notebook with writing was found on the floor of Rob's bedroom near a wooden-handled knife. Police also took a pink blanket off the floor that had several hairs on it.

Two "home made posters" were taken off the east wall of Rob's bedroom. One of the posters was drawn on the back of a map.

Rob's room contained a moderate amount of clothing,

much of which was piled on top of his bed and in contact with the bed linens. Detective Sergeant Keefe also found a cardboard box containing what appeared to be more of the boy's clothing in the hallway outside Rob's room. This was taken away for lab analysis. Police also seized a black fleece pullover from a chair in the hallway outside Rob's room, and a pair of jeans from a clothesline on the first floor.

Detectives going through Tulloch's room reported spotting several books and other documents in full view, including the book *Der Fuehrer*, which dealt with Germany and the Holocaust. They also noticed literature that made some reference to the Ku Klux Klan and "interactive video games known to be violent." Police hadn't asked for specific authority to seize hate literature in their initial search warrant application, so detectives were sent back to court to get an additional warrant for subversive literature, just to be on the safe side.

After the main search of the Tullochs' residence, police obtained a third search warrant to seize Rob's Macintosh computer and another warrant for Rob himself that would allow them to examine and photograph the cut to his right knee, provided they could find him.

It was midnight on Saturday before investigators finally left the Tulloch household carrying more than thirty paper bags of evidence that they had seized.

chapter 22

By now, pictures of Robert Tulloch and James Parker were appearing on the front pages of newspapers across New England, and being featured on newscasts nationwide. But police would go two days before the next sighting of the pair—and that lead would be thirty-six hours old when it was confirmed.

At around 10:20 A.M. on Sunday morning, February 18, Massachusetts State Police Trooper Walter Coombs was looping through the parking lots behind the Sturbridge Isle truck stop off Interstate 84 when he spotted a car that looked like it had been partially, perhaps deliberately, buried in the snow.

It was a silver Audi with a Vermont license plate, and Coombs thought it was an odd plate to see in the employee parking lot of a business that sat just two miles into Massachusetts from the Connecticut border.

Run through the National Crime Information Computer system maintained by the FBI, Vermont plate CDG690 came back as a "hit." It was Parker and Tulloch's getaway car, and it was parked a stone's throw from the truck stop's fueling depot. As Coombs radioed in the information, it became clear to investigators looking at the map that the boys were now probably somewhere on a tractor-trailer headed across the country.

FBI agents and Massachusetts State Police detectives began to converge on the Sturbridge Isle. Unlike a stereotypical modern, flat truck stop, the Sturbridge Isle is a big ornate barn-like structure that sits beside a pond ringed in willow trees. Handsome on the outside, with gabled windows and a spire, and big heavy timber beams, inside it's more like a small downscale country club than a truck stop. There's a gift shop instead of a convenience store; there's a restaurant with a large vaulted ceiling; and in the basement, there is a lounge for truckers, filled with video games, laundry machines, and a shower room.

It had been two days, but employees at the Sturbridge Isle knew exactly who the agents meant when they started asking if anyone remembered two boys looking for rides.

Joe Paquette, a 17-year-old cook at the restaurant, told Trooper Brian Brooks that he had seen the boys getting out of the silver Audi at about 4:00 P.M. on Friday and putting on their backpacks. He remembered the time clearly because he was just coming in to work for the evening, and he also remembered seeing them again an hour and a half later as they were brushing their teeth in the men's room at the restaurant. Paquette was able to identify both teens from the photographs of Tulloch and Parker that Brooks had with him.

Others at the truck stop also clearly remembered the boys hanging around that Friday afternoon.

Inside at the fuel desk where all the truckers pay for their gas, "fuel jockey" Nick Palmerino, a 25-year-old from nearby Southbridge who likes to work with a bandanna wrapped around his head like a pirate, spotted Tulloch and Parker right away and thought they were out of place.

"I saw them for like five minutes," said Palmerino. "Two kids walking around dressed like they were was kind of noticeable. I watched them because they didn't look like truck drivers. They weren't dressed grubby. They were definitely preppy. They were walking in and out of the trucks out here wearing running pants and sweatshirts. One had kinda spiked hair and the other was wearing a hat."

Back at the fuel desk, Nick's friend, fuel clerk Russ Cote, asked him if they should go out and shoo the kids off, but they eventually decided against it.

"It was about a half an hour before we were going to

leave," recalled Cote. "We wondered if we should warn them that the police came around checking the area a lot, and they were going to get in trouble if they found them hanging around the trucks," said Cote, a 26-year-old from Southbridge whose friends call him "Red" because of his distinctive wispy red hair and goatee. "It was like, 'Hey, there's a couple kids outside. Should we say something to them?" Cote said. "They just seemed like a couple kids drifting through on their way to a rock concert or something, and we decided, since we were about to go off shift, to just leave them alone."

After seeing the suspicious reaction they received for hanging around the large trucks, Tulloch and Parker apparently decided they would have better luck if they went into the main building and tried to scrounge up a ride there.

Inside, several waitresses saw the boys purchase toothbrushes in the gift shop, and kept noticing as the pair wandered back and forth around the building for several hours, nervously asking truckers if they could get a ride across the country. Sometime during the day, Parker had gelled his hair up in spikes and Tulloch had dyed his dark hair a sandy blonde and slapped a brown ski cap on his head. The pair smoked cigarettes and drank coffee, but mostly they looked nervously out the windows for someone they might be able to hit up for a ride.

As the hours ticked away, the boys began to realize that, even though they were dressed in northern New England's idea of casual high school clothes, they were increasingly standing out amidst the constant turnover of working-class Massachusetts teens, bedraggled interstate travelers, elderly locals out for dinner, and ball cap–wearing truckers who shuffled in and out every few minutes.

It had gotten dark and the wait staff noticed one of the boys quickly pacing back and forth by the bank of windows facing the truck parking area. They thought the pair seemed awfully young to be out on their own looking for cross-country rides. By 8 P.M., waitresses had begun discussing amongst themselves whether or not the boys were runaways and the police should be called. Waitress Sharon Palmer had seen the boys go into the men's room and she asked a trucker to go in and see if he could overhear what they were discussing. When he checked, the boys were gone.

Late in the game, after they had already aroused considerable interest in their presence on the main floor of Sturbridge Isle, Parker and Tulloch had finally figured out that there was a truckers' lounge down in the basement, and realized that that would be the best place to wait out of sight and casually inquire about getting a ride.

The boys disappeared downstairs and sat in front of a giant wide-screen TV in a small room whose walls were covered with hundreds of ball caps bearing the logos of trucking companies. There they spent the rest of the evening quietly watching movies and trying to strike up conversations with the truckers who trickled through on their way to use the laundry and the showers.

Just outside the lounge, at the shower room check-in counter, Marie Quattrocelli, a 73-year-old resident of Holland, Massachusetts, listened as the boys, who were now giving their names as "Sam" and "Tyler," asked trucker after trucker if they would be willing to give them a lift out to California.

Sometime before 11 P.M. Friday night, someone agreed to take them as far as New Jersey.

As police in Massachusetts were towing the Audi out of the parking lot of Sturbridge Isle to the nearby Sturbridge State Police Barracks, the FBI was calling trucking associations and dispatchers across the East and asking them to be watchful for two teenage boys traveling together, who might be armed and extremely dangerous.

During this process, the FBI learned that at 10 P.M. on Saturday night there had been a sighting of two boys matching the description of the fugitives at the Travelcenters of America truck stop in Columbia, New Jersey. By late Sunday afternoon, FBI agents had saturated that truck stop, which sits astride Interstate 80 just a few miles from the border with Pennsylvania. Agents began showing photos of Tulloch and Parker to truckers and the employees and several people remembered seeing them.

The agents learned that the husband-and-wife trucking team who had picked up the boys in Sturbridge were named Rowdy and Nancy Lee Tucker. Pennsylvania State Trooper Darrell Hubert was able to locate and interview the Tuckers a few hours later. From what he learned, it sounded as though the boys were making up their cover story as they went.

The Tuckers told Trooper Hubert that "Sam" and "Tyler" had wanted to go to Southern California to get jobs on a boat. Impressed with the articulate, clean-cut pair, the Tuckers had given them twenty dollars for meals before dropping them off in Columbia, and had provided them with the number of Nancy's sister, Madeline Lee Bray, in Modesto, California. They suggested that the boys look her up once they got out there and see if she could help them out in their job search.

After the FBI told Tucker that the pair were wanted for a double homicide carried out with tactical combat knives, she had to put in an urgent "Oh, by the way . . ." call to Madeline, and warn her that Tulloch and Parker had her phone number and might well be planning to find her. The phone listing Tucker had given the boys was actually that of Bill Ross, a friend of Bray's, whom she was staying with. "I was a little irate, to say the least, when I heard they had my number," Ross told the Associated Press.

Employees at the New Jersey truck stop remembered "Sam and Tyler" telling people that they were originally from California, but had recently traveled to Salem, Massachusetts, to get jobs. Finding none, they said, they were now trying to get back home.

As the evening wore on, Tulloch and Parker would find another truck to ride. It would be the last leg of their journey.

chapter 23

James Hicks, a sad-eyed 45-year-old trucker from Sumter, South Carolina, with a graying walrus mustache, was having a bad year.

In August, he had lost his job as a part-time security officer for Sumter District 17 after he pled guilty to taking personal trips at district expense. He was sentenced to five years of probation and ordered to repay $32,000.

In October, his 14-year-old son was killed in a dirt bike accident.

Hicks hadn't been scheduled to work the weekend, but he decided to take on a last minute assignment and haul a truckload of M&M candies as far as Chicago.

When he approached Columbia, New Jersey, late that Saturday evening, he heard two teen boys practically pleading for a ride "home" to California on a CB radio they had borrowed at the truck stop.

The teens on the radio sounded exhausted and, missing his surviving 13- and 17-year-old sons at home, Hicks figured he might like the company as he headed West.

"I got three boys; one's in heaven and two are still here, and I just felt sorry for them," Hicks later explained.

Still leery, he keyed the radio and asked the last truckers they had ridden with if they could vouch for the boys. When the Tuckers said that the two hadn't been a problem on the ride down to Columbia, Hicks gave in and offered the kid a lift. In all the years Hicks had been driving trucks, Tulloch and Parker were the only riders he'd ever picked up.

Dog-tired, the two teens thanked Hicks and climbed into the back of his big blue Freightliner with their backpacks.

He tried to strike up a conversation as they rolled off into the Pennsylvania night on Interstate 80, but the boys were simply too worn out. Hicks asked if they missed their parents. "Not really," they replied. Hicks hadn't even gotten their names when they fell asleep on the top bunk of the sleeper cab.

Hicks had a VCR in the truck and had been watching tapes instead of television for the last several days, so he had no idea that FBI agents and local police were scouring the interstates looking for two teen boys traveling together.

Around 2 A.M. on Monday, the boys awoke and asked if there was any food in the truck. Hicks passed them back bags of chips and cans of soda. A couple hours later, realizing that he was approaching Indianapolis and would soon be making the final run over to Chicago, Hicks got on his CB radio and started asking if there were any other truckers heading farther West to whom he could hand off the teens.

Tulloch and Parker were now over 700 miles from home but at that moment a satellite 22,400 miles above them was beaming their pictures down across Indiana on CNN Headline News.

Watching CNN on the television at the brand-new Flying J truck stop just south of New Castle, Indiana, astride Interstate 70 and about 45 miles east of Indianapolis, was Henry County Sheriff's Department Sergeant William Ward.

chapter 24

Sergeant William Ward is one of those small-town police officers who likes to keep track of the big stories . . . just in case they come his way.

As Presidents' Day, February 19, began, Ward was seated at the spanking-new counters of the Flying J truck stop having a 3:30 A.M. "lunch" on his night shift with fellow deputy Landon Dean and Explorer Scout Nathan Neal.

CNN began showing pictures of Tulloch and Parker, and reporting that the pair had been spotted in New Jersey, and were believed to be heading West towards California by hitchhiking with truckers. With I-70, one of the nation's main East–West highways, just outside the door, Ward perked up.

It was Deputy Chris Newkirk's night off, but he couldn't sleep, so he had come in to have ice cream with Ward and Dean while they ate their mid-shift meal. Ward, the self-described "news junkie" of the bunch, explained the Dartmouth murders to the other two. It was the first Newkirk had heard of the case.

The trio broke up, and at 3:45 A.M. the deputies headed back out onto the road to patrol the county. On previous occasions, Sergeant Ward, a 22-year veteran of the sheriff's department, had been clued in to drunk drivers by monitoring the CB in his cruiser, and had once even captured an armed robbery suspect that way, so he turned it on again to see if he could pick up any radio traffic about the fugitive teens. Amazingly, what he heard was James Hicks calling out into the night saying he had two boys who needed a ride to California.

"Can anybody give a ride to two boys from New Jersey who want to go to California?" Hicks asked. "Sure, I can!" Ward answered back, pretending to be a fellow trucker. "Just drop them off at the fuel desk at the Flying J and someone will pick them up in a few minutes," he continued.

Hicks agreed, and Ward slammed his cruiser around in a tight turn and headed back towards the truck stop.

Ward immediately called back to his dispatcher, who happened to be Deputy Landon Dean's wife Kelly, and asked her to pull up the descriptions and other information on the teens who were wanted out of Vermont. Kelly Dean advised Ward that she had just gotten a call from another trucker at the Flying J who had overheard Hicks on his CB, and who thought these could possibly be the teens wanted in the New Hampshire double homicide.

Deputies Dean and Newkirk had heard Ward's exchange with Hicks and with Central Dispatch, and they also reversed course back to the Flying J.

Hicks actually reached the truck stop first, and, as he said farewell to Tulloch and Parker and wished them luck, he gave them a ten-dollar bill for breakfast. The boys thanked him and, not sure exactly which truck was supposed to pick them up, began walking out around the west fuel pump island, headed for the row of tractor-trailer rigs idling beyond.

Ward swung his cruiser into the lot, where he was promptly flagged down by the trucker who had just phoned the tip in to Kelly Dean at Central Dispatch. As the trucker pointed towards the west fuel pumps, Dean and Newkirk pulled their marked cruisers up to the boys and hopped quickly out to begin talking with them. Ward immediately recognized Tulloch and Parker from their driver's license photos, which he had seen broadcast on CNN less than a half-hour before.

Ward drove straight over and joined the other deputies,

who were barraging the teens with simple questions.

Parker and Tulloch were standing in the pre-dawn darkness next to the fuel pumps, wearing multiple layers of pants and sweatshirts with their backpacks on the ground beside them. They had been frozen like deer in the headlights by the abrupt appearance of the deputies, and they were rapidly coming unglued under the intense questioning by the suspicious officers.

Asked his name, Parker replied, "Tyler J. Jones."

"What does the 'J' stand for?" asked Sergeant Ward.

Parker paused a moment and thought, before answering, "Jeffrey."

"What's your birthdate?" Ward continued.

"04"-"03"-"82," Parker replied, pausing between each set of fictitious numbers.

"Where are you from?" Ward pressed.

"Encino, California," Parker replied.

"Spell it," Ward demanded. Parker couldn't.

Tulloch was asked his Social Security number, but said he didn't recall it.

"What's your birthday?" Deputy Dean asked. "May 40th, 1982," Tulloch stammered in all seriousness.

At this point, back at Henry County Dispatch, Kelly Dean had the information from the FBI fugitive bulletin up on the screen of her police computer, and she began reading it out to the deputies. "Robert Tulloch, seventeen years of age, six foot-one, 165 pounds, brown hair, blue eyes . . ." Dean's voice came over the speakers in the cruisers and the portable radios the deputies were wearing.

"That's me," Tulloch announced. "You've got us."

Standing in front of his truck, Hicks watched in amazement as the officers turned the boys around and snapped handcuffs on both of them.

Once the teens were placed in the back of the cruisers, Hicks walked over and asked the deputies why they had been arrested. "They stabbed two professors to death in New Hampshire," was the reply. Hicks shook his head in wonder and then, as he walked back to his truck, thinking that he was lucky to be alive, he began to get angry.

Turning back to the deputies, he told them he had just given the boys ten dollars for breakfast and wanted it back. "There's free food in jail," Hicks said. The deputies nodded and retrieved the money. As the cruiser pulled away, one of the boys leaned towards the window and said to Hicks, "I'm sorry."

"It was just a long shot," Ward told reporters after the arrests. "I didn't expect it would be them."

It was a long shot that paid off for Sergeant Ward and the Henry County Deputies.

It was a long ride that cost James Hicks his job with Marten Transport when the company saw news reports that he had picked up riders against their strict policy forbidding such actions.

"I'm not upset at the company. Their policy is as plain as day. I have no regrets," Hicks told *The Boston Globe* as he prepared to board a bus for the ride back home to South Carolina. "Everything seemed so set up for them to be captured here, maybe it's the way it was supposed to happen. I actually feel lucky."

Tulloch was placed in the back of Deputy Dean's cruiser while Dean picked up the blue-and-black Lowe Alpine Systems backpack which had "Tulloch" handwritten on it in black marker.

Parker was put in the back of Sergeant Ward's cruiser, along with his purple, yellow, and black Jansport backpack. Ward asked if the boys had any weapons, and Parker replied that there was a camping ax in his pack. As they drove into the Indiana night, Parker asked where they were going. "The Henry County Jail," Ward replied. "Are you James Parker?" Ward asked. "Yeah," Jimmy sighed. Ward told him that he wasn't concerned with anything that had happened elsewhere, and if Jimmy wanted to talk to anyone about it, he should wait until he met with investigators. Parker nodded in agreement.

chapter 25

Back in New Hampshire, officials were ecstatic that the suspects were in custody. It had only been three days since the *Boston Globe* affair article had focused suspicion down on the Dartmouth campus even harder, and now authorities had captured two suspects who appeared to have nothing to do with the college.

Although still immensely sad over the circumstances, students and faculty alike at Dartmouth were visibly relieved that they no longer had to harbor dark suspicions about their friends and co-workers.

Attorney General McLaughlin greeted the press at a packed briefing over the noon hour at the Hanover Police Station. He began by saying, "I have spoken with Mariana Zantop in New York this morning, and hope to speak with Veronika shortly. I have confirmed to Mariana that this morning at 4 o'clock, off Interstate 70 at an intersection with Route 3 in Indiana, Henry County, Indiana, sheriffs took into custody the two young men whom we have been seeking."

McLaughlin continued, "I spoke about an hour and a half ago with Sheriff Kim Cronk, who is the High Sheriff of Henry County, Indiana, and expressed to him our extraordinary appreciation for the good work of his deputies. I also had occasion to speak personally with Sergeant William Ward of the Henry County Sheriffs who was the sergeant in charge at the time these two young men were taken into custody. He was in company at that time with Deputy Landon Dean and Deputy Chris Newkirk. I spoke to Ser-

geant Ward at some length about the circumstances that led
to this arrest.

"What I found remarkable in speaking to Sergeant Ward
was how normal and how uncommon he thought this extraordinary service was. I think you can appreciate the sense
of obligation that all of us here have toward this case, that
we all want to especially thank those deputies for what they
did this morning, and Sheriff Kim Cronk for the excellent
way that he has cooperated with us. At the present time we
have both prosecutors from my office, and major crimes
investigators from the New Hampshire State Police, in transit to Indiana, and I would expect they would be there mid-
afternoon," McLaughlin said.

McLaughlin also credited the media with helping to
catch the suspects once they fled. "The truckers were all
watching the same media that we watch, and in that sense,
I think the media really is responsible for the fact that this
particular sheriff out in Indiana was aware of the identity
of these youngsters. He commented to me that he had seen
a CNN broadcast shortly before going on duty," Mc-
Laughlin said.

John Pistol, the Assistant Special Agent in charge of the
FBI's Boston office, next took the podium and told reporters that the FBI wasn't far behind the teens when they were
apprehended. "We had dozens of agents on this. It was a
very high priority for us," Pistol said, adding, "There has
been extraordinary cooperation between law enforcement
and American citizens who came together to help locate
these two individuals. The Hanover Homicide Task Force
has gone to extraordinary lengths, literally working around
the clock, to locate these two individuals.

"We want to thank the members of the trucking industry
for the extraordinary cooperation in helping us not only
locate specifically where these two individuals have been,
and traveled, but the exact locations and times that we were
able to piece together, with the trucking industry's assis-

tance, that enabled us to track these individuals down eventually to Indiana," Pistol said.

"We had pursued the leads through Massachusetts to a truck stop in New Jersey. FBI agents went physically to the truck stop in New Jersey and interviewed truckers and people at the truck stop who had seen the two individuals, and, based on that information, pursued it through Pennsylvania and presumably through Ohio, and on into Indiana. We were tracking the information that the attorney general mentioned about California and the logical routes out that way, the Ohio Turnpike and Interstate 70," Pistol said.

With the identification and capture of the suspects out of the way, the assembled press corps turned back to the question looming over the entire investigation: Why had the Zantops been killed?

Officials simply didn't have an answer.

Asked if the investigators had found any links between Tulloch and Parker and either of the Zantops, McLaughlin said, "We are continuing to work on the issue of connection. We are continuing to investigate the connection. This is certainly a remarkable turning point in this case, but for us, the investigation continues and each time we develop new information, it posits new questions . . . our obligation is to try to find the answer to those questions, so for us, in very real respects, this is an ongoing investigation."

Pressed to describe, even generally, a motive in this case, McLaughlin bristled, "I would never for a second think that they didn't have a motive. I think the problem is that we are continuing to investigate to try and determine what the motive is. I'm not intending to be flippant, but this is not *Law & Order*, we don't do this in thirty-five minutes. We do this at the pace the information comes to us. Sometimes that can take weeks, sometimes it can take years. In this instance, I'm simply pleased that it has taken the relatively short time that it has, and we will continue to investigate until we get the maximum amount of information that we are able to get."

If it hadn't been for Trooper West and Detective Moran's effort to sift through thousands of knife sales, the two teens would probably have been sitting in high school that morning, and although he wasn't yet prepared to release details, McLaughlin and New Hampshire State Police Colonel Gary Sloper obliquely acknowledged that fact to reporters during the conference.

"What led us to the two young men was excellent forensic investigation and follow-up investigation by police authorities," said McLaughlin.

Colonel Sloper added, "It all came down to hard-nosed police work and dogged determination on the part of all the investigators, and that's the only reason we've come to this conclusion at today's date."

"This is a turning point in this particular case," McLaughlin continued. "The investigation into the deaths of the Zantops has gotten to a critical point. We have identified youngsters who we think are responsible, and we have apprehended them, and now we will begin the prosecutorial phase of the case," he said.

When reporters asked McLaughlin to expand on reports that had moved over the news wires saying that it had been fingerprints on knife sheaths which had tied the teen suspects to the Zantop scene, McLaughlin bristled and asked the assembled reporters, "What was the source of that report?"

It had come from Orange County Sheriff Dennis McClure, who had read it off the search warrants that New Hampshire detectives had filed with the Orange County Court, documents that, in Vermont, are routinely released to reporters, and considered public information.

"All I know is that the prints [from the crime scene] probably matched enough for an identification," McClure told the Associated Press.

Told that McClure was the source, McLaughlin replied, "That sheriff did not distinguish himself as a professional," and went on to the next question.

It was a remark that was widely reported and which caused considerable anger around the Orange Country Sheriff's Office where McClure and the deputies felt they had been left out of the loop by New Hampshire authorities from the start. McClure would later tell reporters that the whole three-day nationwide manhunt might well have been avoided if officials had just asked his department to keep the suspects under surveillance after the New Hampshire authorities heated them up that night with the dual set of interviews.

McClure said the first official confirmation he had that the Chelsea boys were wanted in connection with the homicides, and were considered armed and dangerous, came when the nationwide teletype printed out in his office, and every other police department in the Northeast, on Saturday.

"One of the problems with this case was that the attorney general in New Hampshire put a gag order out when he should have let some of the information go that wouldn't have been that detrimental to the case," says former Orange County Sheriff Sam Frank. "Everybody supposedly knew it anyway, and that would have kept this thing from just being a news frenzy. He did more damage to the case by keeping his mouth shut than if he had given some of the information out, and then he dumped on McClure. He was out of line on that, because McClure did absolutely nothing wrong," Frank said.

Whatever the bad feelings behind the scenes with their neighbors in Vermont, the New Hampshire authorities had delivered a set of suspects to a community that had begun to think the investigation was stalled and might never identify a perpetrator.

McLaughlin seized the moment. "My office and the Major Crimes Unit of the state police deal every single day with homicides. We have probably twenty to twenty-five homicides a year, but they occur with sufficient frequency to bring a lot of grief to the people of this small state. In that sense, I think we view them all very, very similarly. Here, obviously, the circumstances differ because of the notoriety of the individuals who were killed, and I think we all feel the same sense of gratification when we solve homicides. Gratification in the sense that we've resolved issues of public safety, we are doing the job that we are expected to do, and I must say there is some special connection between my office, and the Major Crimes Unit, and the family members of the individuals who have been taken, and that is always a compelling experience. There is a sense of moral obligation that I think we feel we owe to them.

"There is a certain air of satisfaction being here today when we can actually report that we have suspects in custody, but I try to bear in mind that for the daughters of Mr. and Mrs. Zantop, time stopped on January twenty-seventh," McLaughlin continued. "I'm sure they share approval for what's occurred here today, but I sense in a deeper way that this is small comfort for the losses that they have sustained. I think that all of us, as human beings, can appreciate that any time anyone in the state of New Hampshire is taken, that it is a personal loss. I think we should also acknowledge that there is simply no way for us to appreciate the loss to these two young women of the people whom in this life they loved the most, and cared for the most."

chapter 26

Across the Connecticut River in Vermont, the initial reaction from Chelsea seemed to be one of flat-out disbelief. Townsperson after townsperson expressed shock that two of "their" boys had been implicated. As the wave of reporters followed on the wave of police, the initial reaction at the town gathering spots was: No way. Not them. Not here.

On first glance, Vermont can be a bit deceptive. It's probably the only state that really looks like its postcards from one end to the other; but hidden amongst its endlessly green mountains, charming little villages, picturesque dairy farms, ski resorts, horse riding associations, cider mills, and Ben & Jerry's ice cream factories there are enough small pockets of squalor and nastiness to keep daytime television busy for years.

If you know where to look around Vermont, you can find plenty of "bad neighborhoods." Sometimes they are actual neighborhoods in a small city, sometimes just a few specific streets in a small village, sometimes just a collection of trailers at the end of a dirt road woven right in with breathtaking natural scenery.

There have always been farm boys who liked to bring their girlfriends up to the tops of Vermont's forested Class IV dirt roads for late-night bonfires and beer busts, but in recent years the problems have gone way beyond that. Into certain Third World pockets of Vermont are tucked endless varieties of teens and adults who dress like urban thugs and make frequent trips down Interstate 91 to places like Lawrence, Massachusetts, and New Haven, Connecticut, and return with enough heroin and other entertainments to fuel the party along for another week.

Once in a while, these kids will get together and break into the local stock of seasonal homes . . . partying, looting, and trashing the places before moving on to the next target. On an average weekend, plenty of Vermont's county sheriffs are quietly transporting kids from homes that have been shattered by drinking, drugs, and family fights to temporary foster care placements in a cycle that doesn't seem to diminish with time.

When authorities announced that they were seeking two Vermont teens for the Dartmouth killings, there were plenty of people familiar with the bleaker side of Vermont who nodded their heads and immediately developed a mental picture of the kind of kids the authorities must be talking about.

They were wrong. Tulloch and Parker didn't fit the stereotype, and Chelsea wasn't that kind of town.

There's no shortage of pretty little villages in Vermont, but Chelsea is certainly one of the prettiest. It sits in a narrow north–south valley where the head of the First Branch of the White River winds through as little more than a quiet mountain stream. The houses and buildings clustered within the village lie mostly along a straight single mile of Route 110 that becomes Main Street as it passes through. Many of the homes in Chelsea date from the turn of the last century or before, and are excellent examples of the simple Victorian wood or brick Federal styles with the traditional peaked roofs and wooden shutters that define much of Vermont. On either side of the village, steep green hills rise another nine hundred feet. The small village of Chelsea is the heart and soul of the town that bears the same name, and half the population lives within it. The other half of the residents are spread out through the vaguely defined areas known as East Hill and West Hill on either side, even though in each case, they are really a collection of hills, some with specific names, others without.

Chelsea got its start two decades after Etna, New Hampshire, when the governor of the Freemen of Vermont granted the town its charter in 1781. But like Etna, most of Chelsea's early years were spent in obscurity as handfuls of early settlers traveled up to clear the land and build a town in the wilderness. Unlike Etna, which was never more than a small rural crossroads and mill village, Chelsea aspired to be the county seat, and, after residents drew together and voted to finance the construction of a courthouse, Chelsea was indeed designated as the "shire town" for Orange County.

This was an important distinction in its day, because it meant that, in addition to commercial and trade interests, the village would also become the focal point for all legal transactions in the county, and the nexus of the county's major roads for the next two centuries.

Like almost all villages in northern New England, Chelsea had a town common which was first cleared of trees and rocks for public use in 1794. A church and several other buildings were swiftly built on the larger parcels of land bordering what is today called the "North Common." When it came time to site the new county courthouse, the townspeople ended up having to buy a parcel of land a short distance to the south of the common.

A local resident stepped forward in 1802 and donated another piece of land to form an additional "South Common" in front of the new court building. The two pieces couldn't be linked up into one big common, because a small strip of homes and businesses had already been built down what was now the divider between the two parcels of land. Thus, Chelsea became unique in Vermont for having two distinct "twin commons" just a stone's throw from each other.

Reporters wandering around the twin commons in the first hours after Rob and Jimmy were announced as the suspects had a hard time coming up with a quick, snappy description of Chelsea's reason to be. Initial reports described it as "a logging town." Well, maybe it was one back around 1781 when it was first chartered by homesteaders and land speculators, but by February 2001, there weren't any more loggers in Chelsea than there were scattered throughout the rest of Vermont.

The next try was "dairy farming community," which moved the bar up to about 1958, when there were nearly seventy dairy farms operating in the town of Chelsea, but in the last two decades the number of working farms had dwindled down to nine.

The truth was that the 1,200 residents now living in Chelsea, like those in many East Central Vermont villages today, had become a much more eclectic bunch of people than the plain-spoken Vermonters who built the place.

In fairness to the out-of-state reporters, it can be pretty hard to spot any real diversity in February when the perpetual Vermont winter has turned most year-round residents into extras for a performance of *Ethan Frome*.

To this day there's only one traffic light in all the seven hundred square miles and seventeen towns that make up Orange County, and it's not in Chelsea. But for all its quaintness and supposed isolation, many of the people who have considered Chelsea home for decades nonetheless leave every weekday and drive either north or south to work and to shop in the small Vermont cities of Barre and Montpelier, or in the New Hampshire cities of Lebanon and Hanover.

There is still an agricultural side to Chelsea, and it still has prominence in the tiny village center where the tack shop and Button's store sell supplies, but more local people work in the Vermont government bureaucracy in Montpelier, or at the massive Dartmouth–Hitchcock Medical Center in Lebanon, or building high-speed Acela trains for Amtrak at Bombardier Corporation in Barre, than stay home and tend horses, cows, and sheep in Chelsea.

The Chelsea residents clomping into Will's, the brick general store at the base of the North Common, in their heavy snow boots, jeans, flannel shirts, and weathered jackets, expressing amazement at all the television satellite trucks parked around the village, may have looked a lot alike to the uninitiated, but for all their seeming homogeneity, the residents of Chelsea were not by any means of one mind about what was going on with Robert Tulloch and James Parker.

Vermont always seems to have its waves of immigrants from the real world. In the 1960s, it was the back-to-the-land crowd, who were going to open communes and live in Mongolian-style yurt houses out in the pucker brush. In the 1970s, it was the ski bums who mistook perfectly respectable Yankee hill farms for Switzerland and built little faux Swiss chalets and A-frames around the newly formed resorts. In the 1980s, it was the crowd who had seen the movie *Baby Boom*, and came to Vermont to make jellies and jams with little ribbons tied around the lids for sale on the shelves of the urban areas they had just left. And in the 1990s, it was the high-tech zillionaires from around the country who began quietly designing second homes that were larger than their newly adopted town's municipal buildings, and constructing them at the ends of dirt roads where they couldn't be seen except from space. Regardless of the specific nicknames for new arrivals, there is one over-arching division amongst those who live in the Green Mountains: Those born in the state are Vermonters; anyone born anywhere else is a Flatlander (including people born in New Hampshire—one of the most mountainous states in the country).

Chelsea was one of those towns where a bunch of the 1960s crowd had landed in force.

There's a fundamental old Vermont saying that goes, "Good fences make good neighbors," and it often initially strikes Flatlanders as meaning something along the lines of: Good riddance to anybody who's outside my fence. However, the real meaning is much more subtle. To truly get it, you have to understand that, back when almost all of

Vermont was covered with family farms, it was the legal responsibility of each individual landowner to maintain strong fences that kept their animals on their own property. Many Vermont communities still keep up the tradition of appointing a Board of Fence Viewers (the joke is that it's usually the five oldest guys in the town). Over the centuries in Vermont it was the job of the fence viewers to go out and inspect complaints that a particular landowner hadn't adequately maintained a fence. Thus, the phrase "Good fences make good neighbors" really reflects a Vermont mind-set that, as long as you uphold your share of your community responsibilities and don't cause other people problems, you're all right with the rest of us.

When the "back to the land" group began arriving in Chelsea in the 1960s, there were plenty of people who thought they were nuts, and didn't like aspects of their philosophies (the phrase "sprout-heads" was heard a lot around the state). But once you've come to the annual town meeting a few years running, lived through the winters like everybody else, and learned to shut up about how much damage the milk tanker trucks cause to your roads in the spring, then you are pretty much "in" anywhere in Vermont.

There are certainly plenty of jokes between the two "sides" that run along the lines of "Real Vermonters don't milk goats," but underlying the good-natured name-calling between the "woodchucks" and the "hippies" was a fundamental realization that the old-timers and Vermont's agricultural base were fading. Today even the New Age "trustafarians" (short for "trust fund Rastafarians"), who dreamed of living quaintly among the early-to-bed, early-to-rise dairy farmers, are suddenly finding themselves surrounded more and more by rural-suburbanites who have given up milking cows for nine-to-five jobs.

Chelsea has a tendency to strike adults as a perfect place to bring up children. Meanwhile, it has a tendency to seem to teenagers like they've been trapped somewhere on the dark side of the moon. The last excitement that any of them could remember was in 1996 when a Vermont-based film production company took over the scenic village center for several months to shoot the movie *A Stranger in the Kingdom*, starring Ghostbuster Ernie Hudson.

By the time the new Millennium rolled around, the hippies in Chelsea were largely on par with the natives in terms of voting power, by virtue of three decades in the community, and having put their kids through the local school. They might still be a numerical minority in an overall town census, but in terms of the age group that actively participated in town affairs, they were about fifty-fifty with the rest of the population.

The first word out of Chelsea about Rob Tulloch and Jimmy Parker was that they were both exemplary young men who had never been in any sort of trouble.

Both teens came from two-parent households and had siblings who were well known around town. Both sets of parents were considered solid, even active, members of the community. Both boys seemed to be doing well in school and generally seemed happy being there.

Rob was the president of the student council at Chelsea's tiny high school, and an award-winning debate team member. Jimmy was a gifted young piano and bass guitar player, and a comic student actor who played on the Red Devils basketball team. Jimmy had been away for a semester at a larger high school a half-hour to the north, in the city of Barre, but had recently re-enrolled at Chelsea. Both boys had sailed through physics and advanced math classes and were going to finish earning all the credits needed for graduation a year early.

The thoughts of Robert's fifteen-year-old neighbor, Molly Jackson, who lived right across the street from him, reflected much of the early coverage.

"I just saw Robert in school on Wednesday. He was talking to some people about how he hadn't done anything with the debate team in forever," Molly told reporters, continuing, "Robert and Jimmy have been really good friends for a really long time. They were in the drama club together, and they are both straight-A students.

"Robert is quiet; he's the all-American kind of guy, a really good student. He's smart and he's funny. He was president of the student council last year, and he made a lot of speeches," Molly said, adding, "Jimmy is always the class clown."

Molly's mother Wanda Jackson, who was working at the village general store at the time, echoed her daughter's comments and added that she'd never heard of either boy getting into trouble, not even on Halloween, when pumpkin-smashing and other pranks take center stage throughout the town.

"Robert is in our art class. He spent the whole week modeling a clay head," said student Julia Purcell in an interview with *The Boston Globe*, adding, "After killing someone, no one could do that."

Talking to the *Rutland Herald*, 17-year-old Chelsea senior Torry Hook said she and her classmates examined the Zantop murders in their Current Affairs class the week after the killings. Both Tulloch and Parker were present. "They didn't say anything," Hook said. "It was just, 'Yeah, that's too bad.' "

Coincidentally, several of the other Chelsea students in the drama club had been rehearsing a play called *Juvie* (as in juvenile offender), which dealt with teen violence and murder, when the entire Zantop case suddenly landed on their school. The *Juvie* performance was to have been Chelsea's entry into Vermont's state-wide one-act high school play competition, and, based on that, and the potential for other unfortunate comparisons, Chelsea Principal Patricia Davenport decided to cancel the play entirely, reluctantly bumping the drama club right out of their season.

Reporters asked about drug use, and friends assured them that, when it came to the "prep"-crowd kids like Rob and Jimmy, that idea was ridiculous. In fact, friends described Rob and Jimmy's vehement opposition to any sort of narcotics or even legal artificial stimulants like coffee as "weirdly annoying."

"As far as a dark side like drugs, or even a sexual awakening thing like body piercings or whatever, they didn't seem to have a feel for that," said Chelsea Debate Coach John O'Brien. "They didn't seem like those kind of kids."

"They were very against having drugs, smoking, caffeine, booze," Rob's girlfriend Christiana Usenza assured reporters, adding that, as far as the notion they could have killed someone, "It just doesn't fit with their personalities, their goals. . . . this just doesn't make sense at all."

The reflexive praise of both boys seemed genuine to the reporters who were draining down the coffee and hot chocolate reserves at Will's Store, but at the same time, there was a sense that the media was being spun.

For all the talk about how Rob and Jimmy didn't smoke or even drink coffee, that was exactly what the waitresses and staff at the Sturbridge Isle truck stop had remembered the pair doing just hours after they had fled Chelsea.

Reporters quickly caught wind of the fact that kids at the Chelsea Public School were being coached on how to speak to the press, and being urged to say things like, "Rob and Jimmy are nice people," instead of "I thought Rob and Jimmy were nice people."

Watching New England Cable News from her mother's house in Connecticut, where she had been visiting on the weekend as the manhunt for the fleeing teens was unfolding across the country, was Chelsea Town Constable Carol Olsen. Every half-hour as the headlines rolled, Olsen saw a parade of supporters step up to the microphones singing the praises of Rob and Jimmy over and over. Olsen wasn't buying any of it.

Olsen had arrived in Chelsea in the 60s with the rest of the hippies, but by the time 2001 rolled around, three decades in the Green Mountains had transformed her into a curious mix of New Age space case and no-nonsense Vermonter. Olsen runs a jewelry, gemstone, and crystal healing business but also serves as Deputy Town Clerk, and has now been elected twice to the post of First Constable.

The position of town constable is one of those curiosities left in the Vermont Constitution, along with a couple of dozen others like the Board of Fence Viewers, the Grand Juror, and the Weigher of Coal. These positions can go unnoticed in most towns, but matter in others. The constables were largely eclipsed in the last century, when the cities, towns, and villages that really needed full-time officers started their own police forces. The Vermont State Police now do most of the heavy lifting out in the rural areas, and they are backed up by the sheriffs' departments in the state's thirteen counties.

Still, the constables remain on the books, and have to be elected at each community's annual town meeting in March. In some towns the position is largely ceremonial, and the constables just guard the ballot boxes. In other towns the constables handle stray animals or other specific tasks the townspeople want taken care of. In still others, they have a cruiser with a blue light and function like one-man police forces.

Whatever flavor of constable a town has, the fundamental fact remains that, because they are actually elected by the townspeople, the First Constables and Second Constables are legally the highest-ranking law enforcement officers within the town boundaries.

Constable Olsen beat it back to Chelsea and told reporters she didn't think the teens in question were such great little citizens. Furthermore, she said, there was a group of people in town who were trying to kid themselves into believing that whatever happened in Etna couldn't possibly be a result of the way a larger group of teenagers were being raised around the twin commons.

"I've never represented myself as a trained police officer. I just started speaking as somebody who's got their eyes open and who's been re-elected twice," Olsen explained. "I thought these kids did this and I thought we all needed to be responsible and take a look at this. Let's not pretend like Chelsea's this idyllic little place because everything that is out there is already here . . . all the drugs, all the crime, and the psycho kids who murder people."

On the evening of Thursday, February 22, just three days after Tulloch and Parker were captured in Indiana, a meeting was called by the "Friends of Chelsea School," basically the local PTA, in the white 1812 wooden church at the top of the North Common.

Even though it was billed as a "town meeting–style discussion," reporters and news photographers were barred from the gathering, which was led by local psychiatrist Dr. Andrew Pomerantz. Frustrated news crews stood outside in the dark on the icy sidewalk in the freezing night air for hours, hoping to get someone to stop and talk about what was being said inside. As some of the two hundred attendees began leaving the meeting early, television crews even tried singing the Barney song—"We love you, You love us . . ."—as the heavily bundled townspeople bolted out the big wooden doors of the church and scurried away like mice caught in the camera lights.

The thirty reporters and cameramen, who were mainly just interested in staying alive in the arctic breeze that night, watched in amazement as residents leaving the church rounded the corners of the North Common and ran full-tilt for their houses, as though the media pack was going to suddenly turn and chase them through the pitch dark village.

A few of the calmer residents eventually stopped and talked to reporters as the gathering ended and snow began to blow through the air.

"The session dealt with people just wanting to support each other and . . . just a sense of complete helplessness at first," said Laurel LaFramboise. "We were just discussing what we are up against, and how long it will take, and what we can possibly do to help each other out.

"We are trying to keep a positive outlook, and trying to believe that you are innocent until proven guilty, and that no matter what happens, love should be the number-one thing," she continued.

Asked if she had any connection to the Tullochs or the Parkers, LaFramboise replied, "Oh yeah! Everybody knows everybody here. My daughter's best friend is Jimmy's sister, and my husband has worked for John."

Asked what she thought of the murder accusations against the teens, LaFramboise replied, "I just don't believe that it's true. I refuse to believe that it's true. I just don't think that it's possible. One of the shocking things is that if these boys have done something, then somebody could be knocking on my door and telling me that my son has done something heinous."

Laurel said that she felt the town was taking the arrests personally. "One of my biggest concerns was that I worked just a year ago with Robert Tulloch to put together a teen center, and now I feel a sense of responsibility for failing to get that teen center going, and that was one of the things that we addressed tonight," she said.

LaFramboise described Rob as "very willing to open up to people. He worked with the Grange [an ancient agricultural society that still has members in Vermont], he worked with Friends of Chelsea School trying to get this teen center going. He had great ideas, and he was really motivated to help other teens."

How, then, were the people at the meeting explaining the connection between these two boys and the homicide? LaFramboise was asked. "They aren't. They are just saying it's crazy. It's just crazy," she answered.

Stepping up to the microphones after the meeting concluded, Dr. Pomerantz said the main point of the meeting was, "We need to support each other."

"The meeting focused very much on the children of Chelsea," Pomerantz said. "Our role as parents is to be a source of strength and support for our kids. This is a proud community. We think very highly of our children. We are here to support them. It's been a very hard week or so. It's been very hard on people in Etna in particular."

Not everyone thought highly of the meeting. One of those who left early was Constable Olsen.

"In the first place, hardly anybody went to that meeting, except the people in this group that these kids acted among and their friends from outside towns," Olsen recalled afterwards. "A local lawyer was there encouraging people to get the defense fund going and when the big card came out that we were all supposed to sign for the boys, and people started talking about baking 'em cookies and stuff, like these kids were at camp somewhere, that's when I left with my two friends," Olsen said, adding, "I just could not believe it."

"I've caught a lot of flack for speaking out from their lawyers, who have actually told me that I'm nothing more than a meter maid and the 'lowest of the low' on the law enforcement scale around here," Olsen said. "Actually, under the Vermont Constitution I'm the highest of the high.

"I feel like our town needs to be saved. I'm saying this as somebody who's lived in this town for thirty years and who knows what's going on," Olsen said. "There are kids in this town who do their drugs right under the bridge on Main Street, and we have this whole policy where they get let out of school during the day, which lets them do their drugs right under the bridge.

"Everybody who passed by me at the ballot box at Town Meeting in March when I was overwhelmingly re-elected was saying, 'Good job, somebody's got to speak out,' " Olsen added.

A segment of the Chelsea community had taken the arrest of two local boys personally, and it would take weeks for just the initial shock to wear off around the town. Some residents nearly came to blows in the days after posters announcing a family support fund to help the Tullochs and the Parkers with court expenses were put up in the village's gathering spots. Neighbors split hard over whether the teens should be given the benefit of the doubt before their trials, or whether enough attention was being paid locally to the suffering that had been caused in Hanover and Etna.

As authorities began to leak out information about the evidence they had gathered against the two teens, opinions began to shift rapidly in Chelsea. At first, the only link seemed to be that the boys had bought the same brand of knife that had been used in the killings; but then came word that the knives had been found in a box under Robert's bed, and that the police labs had found traces of the Zantops' blood still on them. Next, townspeople familiar with the situation revealed that Rob and Jimmy had landed in the local court's juvenile diversion program the previous summer for their role in at least one breaking and entering. By the time the spring of 2001 gave way to summer, more and more people in Chelsea came forward and quietly began to discuss aspects of both boys that contrasted sharply with the preppy, straight-A class clowns that had been the initial story around the twin commons.

There aren't too many ordinary teenagers in small towns who could expect to have all the publicly stated details of their lives emerge unscathed from the kind of scrutiny that over seventy experienced crime reporters could suddenly put to them. So it was against that backdrop that the press corps covering the Zantop story had to sort out the nuances of what was being said about Robert Tulloch and Jimmy Parker.

A lot of younger kids at the school looked up to Rob and Jimmy as really funny guys who still managed to get straight A's while skipping large hunks of the school year. A lot of the older kids who were actually in Rob and Jimmy's classes knew the pair were smart, but also knew they weren't even close to scoring straight A's because they couldn't seem to stop screwing around. Some students thought the pair were a riot when they cut up in class. Some thought their humor came at the expense of others, and betrayed a fundamental arrogance that they found deeply irritating. In short, it was the normal mix of opinions that adults asking hard questions could find in any high school if they lifted the lid and looked underneath.

But for the fact that they had been named as the prime suspects in a double homicide and chased across the country by the FBI, there was little, even in hindsight, that suggested Tulloch and Parker were anything other than the all-American boys their defenders initially declared them to be after the pair had been fingered by police.

But as the weeks went by, a picture would emerge that began to cast both boys in a slightly different, more confusing light.

chapter 27

While Robert Tulloch and Jimmy Parker had known each other for years, it became clear to others at the start of Tulloch's senior year in the fall of 2000 that the two were now best friends.

To be sure, there were certainly other close friends that both boys hung around with on a regular basis, but when they were together, they were something of a unique entity.

Of the pair, Rob was clearly the leader and the deeper thinker. Jimmy always seemed ready to do whatever Rob thought up, and was eager to go to wilder and zanier levels.

As with a lot of teenage boys, it was a little hard to tell in retrospect what the pair actually did that was crazy and outrageous, versus what they simply told others they had done.

There was a story around town that the boys had taken their interest in rock climbing as far as rappelling off the back of the State House in Montpelier. Others said the pair had scaled the old 1847 Orange County Courthouse on the South Common one dark night.

Neighbors around Jimmy Parker's house noticed a lot of paintball splats in their woods, and sometimes on their property, and they spoke to John Parker about it, after which the stains seemed to diminish.

Residents spotted Jimmy and Robert tearing around back roads in Jimmy's little silver Audi at speeds approaching liftoff. The Orange County Sheriff's Department spoke to Jimmy about it several times, and even nailed him with a ticket on one occasion, but it didn't seem to slow him down.

Robert Tulloch had two older sisters and a younger brother. Becky Tulloch, now 24-year-old Rebecca Johnson, married a local boy from a long-standing Chelsea family, and by all accounts blended well into the community. Julia, 19, is developmentally disabled, and recently graduated from a special school in the nearby town of Hartford. Kienan, 16, is considered well-liked, but is noticeably calmer and more easy-going than his somewhat frenetic older brother.

His father Michael is a finish carpenter with his own workshop in an antique mill building that sits next to the family's distinctive house right in the middle of the village of Chelsea.

His mother Diane, who, like Mike, is forty-six years old, is a visiting nurse based out of the Gifford Medical Center in the town of Randolph a short distance from Chelsea over the mountains.

"Dianne is a home health nurse, and I'm telling you, she is just fabulous. She would lay down in front of a truck for people," said neighbor Kevin Ellis, a former *Burlington Free Press* reporter who is now a lobbyist in Montpelier. "They've always been kind neighbors to me and my kids. They bring you soup if you break your leg and are laid up in bed. They come to your Christmas party. They are very quiet, salt-of-the-earth people, but they are active in the community. I wouldn't call them boosters, but they are part of the glue that keeps any small Vermont town running," Ellis said.

Rob had spent his early childhood in another central Vermont town called Sharon before the Tulloch family briefly moved to Jensen Beach, Florida, in the early 1990s. In 1995, when they returned to Vermont, they settled in Chelsea and bought the landmark Hood House on Main Street and the old Chelsea Mills building immediately beside it.

The house is so distinctive that the Tullochs give out the

address for UPS deliveries as "The Yellow House on Main Street."

Once the seat of the founders of the Hood dairy empire—a company familiar to New Englanders because of its ubiquitous red oval logo with "Hood" written in it, which covers products in supermarket dairy cases across the region—the William A. Hood house had an extensive local history before the Tullochs purchased it in 1995.

A large yellow "Vermont-vernacular"–style two-story farmhouse with peaked roofs, traditional shutters, and clapboard siding, the house is most notable for the short row of tall pines that screen from the street the large wooden porch that wraps around the front of the house.

After the Hoods moved to Massachusetts, the large house became the Brookhaven Home for Boys in the 1950s and 60s. By the 1980s it had become the Chelsea Outpost of the Vermont State Police.

State troopers assigned to patrol Orange County would spend the night in the bedroom that later became Robert Tulloch's. Downstairs they did their paperwork and processed criminals and drunk drivers in the large first-floor rooms. One of the troopers' girlfriends grew increasingly convinced that the creaky old place was haunted by ghosts, and she eventually became too terrified to venture inside it.

Sitting out behind, off the back corner of the Hood House where the First Branch of the White River winds its way through the village, is the Chelsea Mills building. Looking like a plain wooden two-story house, the small mill is most notable for its odd little front porch with a triangular overhang that has had 'Chelsea Mills' written on it since it was built around 1820.

Once the town's principal grist mill, it was here in the dim, sawdust-filled recesses of the old timber-framed building that Michael Tulloch set up his woodworking shop, making cabinets with power tools to pay the bills, but hand-crafting Windsor chairs using original eighteenth-century antique tools as his passion.

"Building the chairs is a personal and spiritual journey. A modern tool has not been invented which can rival these originals. The tools are perfectly suited for the work they perform," Tulloch told *Valley News* reporter Christine Duggan in a profile on his business that ran just a few weeks before Jimmy Parker ordered the knives. "It is the hand tools that bring the work to a personal level. There is a point, as you mold the wood, when a part of you is going into the chair."

Made out of three different kinds of wood, using centuries-old techniques, Windsor chairs, having descended from the British chairs of the same name, have their own subculture. The American colonists made them with hard maple legs for endurance, with Eastern white pine that could be sculpted into the chairs' distinctive saddle-shaped seats, and with red oak or ash back-spindles connected by a curved piece called a bow. A hand-made Windsor chair can last centuries, a factory-produced model probably just a decade or two.

The wood in the chairs has to be worked on while it's still green, so Tulloch begins each chair with a journey through neighbors' forest lots, picking out and culling suitable trees.

Each Windsor chair takes Tulloch a solid week of hands-on work to finish, and the entire process has kind of a New England–Zen quality to it.

"The transformation process which changes the basic, natural form of the tree into a finished chair is fascinating," Tulloch told Duggan.

Tulloch's mentor in the small world of Windsor chair makers has long been Mike Dunbar, the 54-year-old director of The Windsor Institute, located over near the Atlantic seacoast in Hampton, New Hampshire.

Over the past twenty years, Dunbar has taught over 2,500 craftsmen how to make the chairs that first arrived in this country as English garden furniture back in the 1740s, but which quickly became an early American symbol of grace and, in many public buildings of the time, authority.

Dunbar and his Institute are well known in the field of woodworking. But despite the steady stream of carpenters and cabinet makers that come through its doors, shy, reserved Michael Tulloch stood out as a dedicated professional. "Mike is in the extended family here," Dunbar said. "Not only do we know him, but lots of other people in the woodworking world know him.

"Mike Tulloch first came to us back several years ago, and he's been here numerous times since, so I've gotten to know him very well, and much better than I know a lot of the people who come through here," said Dunbar. "He's helped us in many ways, and he's written for our publication, *The Windsor Chronicles*. He just did a book review in the last issue. Earlier he did an article about his experiences when he went to his daughter's school and showed her and the other kids with disabilities how he makes his chairs. He's one of these guys that I really like coming through the shop, because he's a fellow that gives more than he takes. Mike always makes sure he gives back a full measure.

"Beyond being an extremely friendly guy, and very courteous, he never really says a whole lot about his home life," Dunbar noted. "He's very quiet. He is shy. In some ways he's almost apologetic for his presence, but he's very considerate. He's the type of guy I'm proud to know. He's an interior carpenter, the high end, he's one of the guys that come in and do all the finish work. In the woodworking field he's what would be known as a joiner."

Dunbar never met Rob Tulloch, but he recalled that at the first of the year, just days before the Zantops were killed, Mike had called and wanted to enroll himself and his son in one of the Windsor Institute's classes in the spring. The class was already full, and by the time it rolled around, Rob Tulloch would be in a maximum-security block unable to access even the prison workshop because of his classification as a violent offender.

"We were all in a state of complete and total shock," Mike Dunbar said. "Mike Tulloch is universally liked. You cannot find a nicer guy. If you had said someone in our close circle was going to have this happen in their lives, he is the last person I would have thought of, the very last person, because he is just so very nice."

In January, Mike Tulloch had spent the better part of the week prior to the Zantop murders at a conference in Colonial Williamsburg sponsored by *Fine Woodworking* magazine. Dunbar needed someone to take extra examples of the Institute's chairs to Virginia, and Mike volunteered to ferry several of them down in his pickup truck.

"Unfortunately it rained all the way, and I got a call from him on my cell phone in New Jersey in a snowstorm, and it's Mike assuring me that he had gotten to his brother's house in Pennsylvania and taken the chairs inside so they were protected," recalled Dunbar. "Then he arrives in Williamsburg and calls me again, most apologetically, because they had gotten rained on, but he had taken them into his motel room and wiped each one of them dry. And then, because some of them were water-spotted, he had gone out to a hardware store and bought some finishing products to try and get rid of it. This is the type of guy he is. We are talking about a very considerate guy you would love to know."

Michael Tulloch left Chelsea on Saturday, January 20, exactly a week before the murders, and attended the three-day conference in Colonial Willliamsburg that ran from Monday, January 22, through Wednesday, January 24. He then left on the two-day return drive to Vermont.

When the Tullochs had moved to Chelsea from Florida, Rob was in the fourth grade. He enrolled at the Chelsea Public School, just a couple minutes' walk from his house across the twin commons.

Right off the bat, Rob was tagged as one of the smart

kids in the small school system, where the total enrollment in each grade averages only about sixteen children. His teachers loved the fact that he paid attention and seemed to enjoy learning.

"He was one of those kids—every teacher gets one or two a year—that you say, 'Boy, I wouldn't mind if my classroom was full of kids like this. We could really go places,' " his sixth-grade teacher DeRoss Kellogg told *The Boston Globe*.

As a younger kid, Robert was known around the village as the paper boy who delivered the *Times Argus*. He did such a good job that his neighbors were disappointed when he gave it up as he got older.

By the time Rob hit his junior year in the high school section of the Chelsea Public School, he was seemingly on a roll. He had emerged as a champion debater and was elected president of the student council. Under Chelsea's "block" scheduling system, wherein only three or four classes are taught a semester, but each of which count for a year's credit, he would clearly already have enough credits by the time his junior year ended in the spring of 2000 to have earned a diploma. It was still twelve months away, but Tulloch's senior year was already starting to look like a cakewalk.

"He had enough credits, so he just decided that he was not going to take classes," his friend Kip Battey told the *Rutland Herald*. "It was definitely unusual, especially for a senior."

In the wake of the arrests, there were many glowing reports about both boys, but especially Rob, since he had been elected to lead the student council in his junior year. Normally nobody would have cared to split hairs over his tenure, but soon kids began pointing out to reporters that there were some problems with the impression about Rob that the title "class president" was giving to outsiders. Sure, they said, he'd been elected president. But he ran as a lark, was elected as a joke, and never attended a single student council meeting. His lackadaisical attitude towards the post prompted a half-hearted impeachment effort that failed, partly because no one really cared who did or didn't hold the title in the first place.

Although few people had much of a reason to question his successes at the time, there were those who had taken a close look at Rob, and thought that the foundations under his bright school career were shaky.

"He's a smart kid. He'd be a smart kid anywhere. He was a semi-genius," said Tunbridge, Vermont, filmmaker John O'Brien, adding, "He's one of those guys who probably has a fantastic IQ, but because he's not much of a worker, he probably will never capitalize on all his brains."

O'Brien, who was named one of *People* magazine's most eligible bachelors during 2001, attended the Chelsea Public School as a boy growing up in neighboring Tunbridge. In recent years he had returned there to help coach the debate team. Known locally for his sheep farm and nationally for his quirky Vermont-themed movies, including *Man With a Plan* and *Vermont Is for Lovers*, O'Brien did well on the Chelsea debate team as a high school student before going on to Harvard. When he first met Robert Tulloch, O'Brien was delighted that he might have another future Ivy Leaguer on the team he was now coaching. Soon however, his initial enthusiasm turned to a kind of bemused chagrin.

"Rob was definitely very quick and very witty, and he could comprehend things and speak on his feet in ways that most kids that age couldn't. If he'd really wanted to work, he could have been a great debater or a great anything," O'Brien said.

Kids who knew Rob in junior high remember him hatching plans to be President of the United States, but by the time high school got going, it dawned on everyone that Rob wasn't playing in that ballpark.

Tulloch was privately disappointed in his SAT results, and began to get less and less specific when talking about

future career plans. "I think he realized at some point he
wasn't going to go to an Ivy League college," O'Brien said.
"He was very smart, but he wouldn't do the sort of work
it took to get straight A's. He thought he would just natu-
rally get through everything, so he started to get B's and
B-minuses, and then, being Robert, he started doing all this
research on all these famous people who had never been to
college, or who had dropped out. He was really sort of
justifying where he was at.

"He certainly wasn't a bookworm at school, because he
is just too extroverted," O'Brien laughed. "But I remember
asking him about college, and he had no plans, which surprised me because he was much brighter than a lot of kids
who do go to college."

O'Brien coached Tulloch on the debate team during
Rob's junior year, and watched as he won his first-ever
contest against another school hands-down. After that initial
success, he had a much more checkered debate career as
he worked towards the state championship that was held in
the Vermont State House in March 2000.

"Rob was very gung-ho for debate, and he took to it like
a fish to water. He's sort of made for it in many ways,"
O'Brien said. "He's a very bright guy. He's very outspoken. He thinks he's smarter than most of the other students,
so he has sort of a confidence, or overconfidence, that actually lends itself well to debate. Some people would be
terrified by debate, but he really enjoyed it. He was a natural."

During his first debate, Rob and his close friend and
debate partner Kip Battey won 3–0 against the visiting
school, and Rob won the award for Top Speaker of the
evening. "From then on, things didn't go well, because
while he was probably the most natural debater that I'd ever
had, he's also one of the laziest," O'Brien laughed. "He
didn't apply himself. He wasn't like, 'I'm really good at
this and I could be so much better!' he just thought, 'I'm
good at this and I never have to do any more work.'

"In the next round of debates, he did well, but he didn't blow people away so much, because other people who maybe weren't quite so natural started to work, and started to understand debate, and then caught up to Rob. Debate is partly style but part of it is the content too, and Rob never really bothered with the content."

Marilyn Childs, a long-time speech coach at Chelsea, told the *Rutland Herald* that Tulloch's self-assuredness bordered on cockiness. "He's not like your ordinary Vermont kid," Childs said. "He's got a very good vocabulary. He can talk to anybody. He can switch sides in an argument. He was our top debater. A very eager kid."

In Chelsea, Rob got a lot of mileage for being in the drama club and on the debate team, especially from kids who would have died of stage fright if they were asked to get up and argue a point in a room full of people. But when the Chelsea debate team met up with other teams of sharp, articulate kids from around the state, Rob began to get a reputation as a loose cannon.

"I thought he was a troubled kid, actually," remembered Rutland High School Debate Coach Bill Dritschilo, who had several opportunities to observe Robert Tulloch in action around the state.

"In the debate rounds he was downright cruel to the opposition. He just had no sense of decorum. In a way, when I saw this in hindsight [after Rob's arrest] I said, 'Oh My God, Yeah,' but at the time you meet a lot of kids like that who are kind of strange," Dritschilo said, adding, "He was a very rude sort of kid in the debate rounds. Debate requires bringing evidence and using it to support your positions, and he would come in without anything at all and just insult the other team," Dritschilo said.

Still, Tulloch looked the part. "He was well-groomed. He looked like the typical bright kid that you'd expect on a debate team," Dritschilo said. "He would have some successes. It's not like he lost every round. He was not a bad debater. He had a lot of talent actually, except he sort of pushed the envelope."

Debaters complained vehemently about Tulloch's attitude to several coaches over the course of that year. In one instance, two girls from Hanover High School who visited Chelsea were highly insulted when both Tulloch and Parker ended up judging their match.

The incident embarrassed O'Brien at the time, but he wrote it off to the fact that Parker had unexpectedly shown up and joined Tulloch. "Individually they were both really quite sweet and funny and extroverted," O'Brien recalled. "But whenever they got together, they were definitely much more sort of like two dogs.

"In the Hanover incident, Rob had already won his rounds and there was nobody left at his level to debate, so on the last round I said 'You can be a judge, but you have to be responsible and take this seriously,' and he said that he would. Somehow, after that he had joined up with Jimmy without me knowing, and they had just been total jerks throughout the round," O'Brien recalled. "They had been making faces, and playing tic-tac-toe, and they had just decided these other girls should win automatically. I asked them what had happened, and they just said it had been a travesty because these were novices that were debating.

"Well, these were first tournaments and they can be really painfully bad, but there's no need to be hostile," O'Brien said. "The two Hanover girls came up later and were upset. They were really mad, and I was really embarrassed, and that was part of the reason that I didn't make an all-out effort to get Rob back on the debate team the next year, because he was doing stuff like that more and more, especially when Jimmy was around."

Weeks later, when Tulloch was identified in the newspapers as one of the murder suspects, the Hanover girls would tell their high school friends that, based on their brief encounter with Rob, they had a real hard time believing all the reports about how he was supposedly such a nice guy.

By the time Rob got to the state debate championships in March 2000, it was pretty clear that he wasn't going to win. Still, he managed to be memorable enough by insulting other students and being so flippant that several judges remembered him a year later when he was arrested. In one of the more memorable moments, he made a remark about an Asian-American student he was debating. Tulloch said that his opponent was doing well "because all you people are smart." It struck observers as tantamount to an ethnic slur, and Tulloch's debate partner, who had been paired with him from another school, felt compelled to stop and apologize on Rob's behalf in the middle of the debate.

Even back in town some of Rob's classmates were finding it harder and harder to swallow the better-than-you attitude that Rob was projecting as the months wore on. Still, with only forty kids in the senior class, everyone's a player. Rob was just Rob, and Rob and Jimmy together were just one of those fierce high school friendships that was going to be part of the mix whether or not others liked it.

"Together they were just like kids you've seen a million times in schools, smart, witty, and very quick," O'Brien said. "They could crack most kids up, but at the same time, they had some of those cruel and teasing qualities. They were sort of verbal bullies, but never physical bullies. They weren't the types who beat people up.

"They pissed their friends off some days, and then were cool other days. Like a lot of kids that age they had their good days and their bad days," O'Brien said. "Together, they were real smart-ass types."

Like him or not, the other students in Robert Tulloch's classes had spent years viewing him as the kid who was going somewhere someday . . . literally.

"I know that Robert has always wanted to travel," said Christiana Usenza when she described her friend's goals.

Tulloch had spent the last two years of his high school career telling his friends that he couldn't wait to get out and explore the world. He had plans, vague plans to be sure, but definite plans nonetheless to go somewhere, just about anywhere, outside of Vermont.

He talked incessantly during his junior year of spending his senior year in Europe. He was seemingly so serious about it that he didn't bother to sign up for the senior debate team when school ended in Spring 2000. Why bother? He wasn't going to be there.

"Rob was going to go to Europe. He didn't know where. It was very, very vague," O'Brien said. "Robert kept expecting to go somewhere, but he never seemed to have the money, or even to have made plans.

"It was very odd," O'Brien continued. "It was like he had some hidden agenda, but it was so vague he couldn't even articulate it. He never seemed to know anybody there, and he didn't have a specific country or city in mind.

"It was like France, and Germany, and Austria. It was mentioning places without plans. It wasn't even like he wanted to be Jack Kerouac or a hobo in Europe type of thing—it wasn't even that clear. It was definitely just to get away.

"Robert was supposedly working and doing something, but it was never like, 'I'm focused, I need to earn two thousand dollars,' " said O'Brien. "It was more like two hours on the weekends working for John Parker and earning just enough for rock climbing." Tulloch and Parker worked for Jimmy's dad doing clean-up work at the construction sites where his father was building homes, but to their friends it appeared to be an effort to earn pocket money rather than a serious plan to travel.

Asked why the boys didn't enlist their parents' help in trying to figure out how to swing some sort of study trip or enrollment in an international exchange student program, Usenza replied, "I guess there wasn't money available right now for that kind of thing. I'm sure if they were going to go on a trip, their parents would've wanted them to have it all planned out. It wasn't planned out, and they just didn't want to be stopped."

Robert mentioned going to Paris to some friends. He mentioned going to London to others. He talked of taking a trip to Egypt to climb the pyramids. He spoke of a desire to go on a break and climb the Rocky Mountains and tool around the American Midwest. He wanted to travel to both Australia and New Zealand, and throw in some more rock climbing and wilderness orienteering in the remoter stretches of those distant nations.

When the school year began again in the fall of 2000, he'd gotten himself as far as Burlington a few times over the summer, a whole forty-five minutes up Interstate 89 from Chelsea.

"He kept putting it off, and when I'd see him again in the fall I kept joking, 'Well, you're still here,' and he'd be saying, 'Well, I'm still trying to figure it out,' " O'Brien recalled.

Since Rob and Jimmy had started hanging around at the start of Rob's senior year, Rob soon began to refer to the two of them as planning to travel the world together. But still the whole thing lacked any kind of definition.

Christiana Usenza remembered the plan slowly evolving from a trip abroad, to something that sounded more like a move, to a new life somewhere with Jimmy. "Initially it was an idea to go abroad as a learning experience, to be done through school. Robert was trying to get money from the school from a grant that is there for senior projects. He was maybe going to use that to go and learn, and then come back and present what he had done to the class," Usenza said.

The Chelsea Public School did indeed have some grant money available for senior projects, but most of these were relatively low-key endeavors like demonstrating how to tear down and rebuild a tractor engine or how to put together a wilderness camp. A girl in Tulloch's class, the school's other champion debater, had managed to get herself sent to

Africa to study for part of her senior year, but nobody seemed willing to step forward and pay to send Rob, let alone Rob and Jimmy—a junior whom he happened to be close friends with, who was now attending another school— on what sounded like an all-expenses-paid vacation around the world to go rock climbing.

Tulloch's senior year was a puzzle to his friends and the few adults who were paying close attention. He was by all accounts a bright student, but instead of taking additional classes that might have interested him, he essentially planned a senior year without any class load. With the school's liberal attendance policies he mostly came around for lunch, weekly class meetings, and whatever else suited his fancy. By January, he didn't even have a senior project planned out, much less under way, and that was the one thing all year that he really had to do. Tulloch could have even graduated early and been done with even the pretense of being a student, but he didn't bother to do that either.

One of the main ironies about Rob's plans, that struck even his teenage friends, was that for those who felt stifled by Chelsea, there actually was one really simple way to get out of town and see the world. Go to college.

Three-fourths of the Chelsea Public School's graduating seniors go on to a two- or four-year college. If anybody out of the class should have been able to swing going away to school, maybe not to Harvard, but certainly somewhere more interesting than the South Common, it should have been Robert. However, Rob didn't seem the least bit inter- ested in going on with his education, or even in faking enough of an interest to get accepted to some party school on the far side of the planet, something which, of all people, he seemed capable of doing.

Despite his lack of interest in college, Rob seemed dead serious that he had a global trip coming up, and the more his friends listened to him speak about it, the more it sounded like a permanent move.

"They were raising the money together, and they were

working for it but there wasn't enough. I mean, they didn't personally have enough to go to Europe and start a life yet," Usenza said.

Tulloch was becoming a rare presence at the school, and he was increasingly distanced from life in the town. Friends figured that Tulloch was still planning to head somewhere else in the world, and they got the sense that he had some plan in mind to pay for it that he wasn't willing to discuss.

Usenza said that, when the boys told her on January 31 that they were taking off in the middle of the school year to "start new lives" in Colorado or somewhere, far from being alarmed at the suddenness of the trip, she was under the impression this was the start of the big excursion he had been talking about for over a year.

In the weeks that followed Tulloch's arrest, Christiana Usenza would find herself referred to in press accounts as Rob's "sometime girlfriend," his "on-again, off-again girlfriend," his "occasional girlfriend," and his "long-time friend and girlfriend."

Christiana herself would have a bit of a hard time characterizing her relationship with Rob. Christiana was just over a year older than Tulloch when they both had met playing soccer on the town rec field. Rob was eleven at the time, but they hit it off and were soon fast friends. They hung out together and played games, and as they got older, Rob would ask Christiana to the prom, and be seen holding hands with her sometimes when kids were sitting around the common.

At a press conference following the boys' arrests, Christiana met with a roomful of reporters at the offices of lobbyists Kimbell Sherman Ellis in downtown Montpelier to describe her relationship with Robert. Dressed in a boxy red jacket, a striped T-shirt, dark blue cargo pants, and wearing red socks that contrasted with her chunky black sneakers with white laces, Usenza faced over a dozen reporters with her mane of thick dark hair swept up in pencil curls over her face and punctuated by sparkly pink minia-

ture hair clips. Usenza came off as poised and impressive
as she told reporters that she had considered herself Rob's
girlfriend at the time of his arrest, but at the same time she
didn't want to give off the impression that it was a torrid
romance. She seemed more comfortable with the term
"close friend."

It was a low-key relationship that many of the adults
who knew Rob missed entirely. "I wasn't around Rob and
Jimmy all that much, but I never saw any sort of hint from
either one of them that they had girlfriends," recalled John
O'Brien.

In her junior year at Chelsea, Christiana had moved out
of her mother's house and gone to live in the Washington,
Vermont, home of family friend Bob Sherman, a former
reporter for the *Times Argus*, who was once press secretary
for Vermont Governor Madeline Kunin, and who was now
Kevin Ellis' partner in their Montpelier lobbying firm. She
switched to Montpelier's high school, which is one of the
most bizarrely named schools in America. It ended up being
called simply "U32" after its district designation number,
because the townspeople nearly came to blows during a
protracted attempt at picking a real name, and finally gave
up in disgust.

Sherman had been acting as her guardian for over a year
when she finished high school, graduating in January just
before the murders.

"I did have a very separate life [from Rob and Jimmy],"
Christiana, now nineteen years old, explained. "I used to
go to school with them and see them every day, but now
my life is based mostly in Montpelier. There were times
when I didn't see them for a week maybe. We didn't always
talk about what we did, but I pretty much knew what they
were up to."

Reporters noticed that it was Christiana whom Rob
called the night that police questioned him, and it was
Christiana he gave his teddy bear to, but it was Jimmy, and
not Christiana, whom he left with.

Christiana also seemed to give conflicting accounts about aspects of the trip that ended in St. Louis.

"You described this as a move out West, they were planning to stay permanently out there?" asked a reporter.

"Yeah, that's what they told me," Christiana said.

A short time later, Christiana was asked if she thought it was strange that Rob and Jimmy just took off on the trip out West on their own in the middle of the school year. Usenza answered, "No. It seemed like just spontaneous fun. 'Let's go out and have an adventure and see what happens.' "

"Is it true that Jimmy's parents had ordered him back because they weren't happy that he'd left?" asked a reporter.

"Um, they told their parents that they'd be gone for a couple of days. And their parents seemed fine with it," Christiana answered.

This contrasted sharply with an answer she had given a couple minutes before at the same press conference.

"Did you have the impression that their parents were aware that they were taking this sudden trip?" a different reporter asked.

"I knew that their parents didn't know," Christiana answered quietly.

The Tullochs apparently had no idea that Rob was headed on a bus across the country in early February, and friends had noticed before that Michael and Dianne Tulloch gave Rob wide latitude to do what he liked and to set his own agenda and schedules.

"Robert's like a freak in his own family, and they probably just don't know how to deal with him," O'Brien noted. "Robert's parents seemed to be really hands-off. It was sort of, 'You're an adult now, you can do what you want.' "

But one area where Michael Tulloch did put his foot down in the weeks before the murders took place was the Internet. Rob was known amongst his friends as the computer whiz you went to see when your system crashed, but in mid-January he told friends that his father had taken away his Internet privileges. Rob explained that his dad had found out he was spending up to six hours a day in chat rooms. Rob didn't tell his friends what kind of chat rooms were involved, but they got the impression that something about their content had disturbed his father.

Christiana Usenza and other friends would tell reporters in the weeks after Rob's arrest that they had never seen any fascination with knives on his or Jimmy's part. However, 16-year-old classmate Clay Tucker II would recall in an interview with the Manchester *Union Leader* that he had seen a drawer full of weapons, including a dart gun, a Ninja throwing-star, and several different kinds of knives, in Tulloch's bedroom back when Rob was about thirteen. "I don't know if he still has them," Tucker told the paper.

chapter 28

Of the Rob and Jimmy duo, it was Jimmy Parker who seemed to be the easier of the pair to figure out.

The most frequent description of Jimmy from classmates at the Chelsea school was that he was the class clown, and a really funny one at that.

Jimmy had spent his entire life in Chelsea. He grew up and went through the local school four years behind his older sister Diana.

His father John Parker is a home builder with a reputation for high-end workmanship. Michael Tulloch had once worked for John Parker.

His mother Joan Parker works part-time as a "paraprofessional" teacher at the Chelsea Public School, helping special education students and doing textile crafts and other projects within the school's Art Department. Around town she is known as the local tennis ace and racquetball champion.

John Parker, who was originally from Poughkeepsie, New York, and Joan, who grew up in San Diego, moved to Vermont in the late 1970s to start a family by, in the words of a friend, "literally taking out a pen and dropping it on a map to pick a place to live."

As a younger kid, Jimmy was viewed mostly as Diana's quiet, overly anxious little brother, and he was frequently teased by some of the older students for his narrowly set eyes. He got roughed around a bit by the older boys, and was considered something of a wimp among the outdoorsy types at the school, even though he played a lot of sports.

In an area where families have been out shooting all

kinds of fuzzy things in the hills for generations, Jimmy had opted out of deer hunting invitations from relatives and friends because he didn't like to camp out, was afraid of the dark, and just couldn't see himself making an animal suffer.

"He was the most anti-violent person," Annette Johnson, the mother-in-law of Tulloch's older sister Becky, told the *Valley News*. "Jimmy could not conceive how he could kill a deer."

Johnson's son coached Jimmy in basketball as a junior high student, and remembered him as being a great player, but at the same time, Jimmy had problems with the way his performance helped defeat the other teams. He didn't like the fact that the opposing players felt bad after losing to Parker and the rest of the victors.

While some adults saw Jimmy as shy and sensitive, others saw him as lonely and adrift.

"Jimmy Parker was this quiet, lost little kid who you could just about count on finding him downtown," Constable Carol Olsen remembered. "When he was younger, I saw him so many times on the pay phone at night, I'm assuming trying to get a ride home.

"Jimmy Parker just basically moved around town and did whatever. His parents were busy. His mother was busy doing her thing, and his father was busy doing his. They are nice people, I always thought John was nice," Olsen continued. "John's done a lot of great stuff, but they weren't there, they didn't know where their kids were, and they didn't know what they were doing.

It was Olsen's view that both of the Parker kids were "truly bizarre" in high school. "His older sister Diana and he were the two kids in the school whose hair was always different colors, which in and of itself isn't like anything major, but it was always weird clothes, some days Diana would go to school with a tutu on, that kind of thing. It was stuff that wasn't necessarily strange if it was like a 15-

year-old kid doing it once in a while, but these kids were trying to be extremely strange all the time.

"The town did not see Rob and Jimmy as great kids," Olsen opined. "We kind of looked at Jimmy Parker as coming from a family where nobody's in charge, there's no discipline, there's no boundaries. These kids were allowed to do whatever they wanted because you don't want to infringe on their creativity, their individuality."

While the Parkers allegedly hands-off parenting style had its detractors, there were also friends who stepped forward to defend John and Joan, saying that the Parkers were caring parents. The Parkers' defenders argued that in a small town, where little if anything could really be expected to go wrong, giving children lots of personal space showed a willingness to let them learn life's lessons directly from their own mistakes and triumphs.

When he reached high school age, Parker's wilder, crazier side gave him a role he could play. He was becoming increasingly musical and his interest in theater and his quick, comic wit were allowing him to stand out in class. When other kids began to refer to him as "the class clown," Jimmy latched onto the label and played it for all it was worth.

Jimmy's favorite movie was the utterly stupid Jim Carrey flick *Ace Ventura, Pet Detective*, and in later years it would be Carrey whom friends would compare Jimmy with when they were fishing for a description of his antics.

"Jimmy was definitely the clown, like everybody said," debate coach John O'Brien noted. "He was always on, and he seemed really lightweight, not a super-deep guy. If you were talking to him, he'd always be making faces or clowning around, almost sort of like Attention Deficit Disorder, a Jim Carrey type of guy, he just couldn't help himself from always trying to make people laugh or doing something weird. I could never imagine just having him sitting still in class and writing an essay, he would always be in the class like drooling on the paper or making spitballs or something."

Parker was a hit in the school's production of *The Importance of Being Earnest*, in which he played the butler. He was also well remembered around town for his performance in one of Chelsea's parades when he dressed as the Big Bad Wolf and chased three little kids costumed as pigs around a float.

By his junior year, Jimmy was still considered a "sports guy," playing hockey regularly in the weekly games in the center of the village and showing up for soccer matches. But as he met with escalating success being the class clown, Jimmy also became more and more flamboyant in the process.

"Jimmy always did crazy stuff just because he could," recalled freshman Molly Jackson. "He'd wear orange-and-pink tropical shirts in the winter just to be funny. He'd disrupt classes all the time, but he'd still make the teachers laugh."

In his sophomore year, Jimmy suddenly appeared with his dark hair dyed blonde. For his junior prom he showed up in full tuxedo and top hat, sporting a cane.

When Jimmy became best friends with Rob Tulloch, a senior to whom it had never occurred that popularity wasn't automatic, some of Rob's over-arching superiority complex began to rub off on his younger friend, and several of Parker's classmates picked up on the fact that he seemed to think they were stupid.

"Nobody liked him at all," recalled Parker's classmate Clay Tucker II in his interview with the Manchester *Union Leader*. "He was always doing stupid stuff to irritate people."

Some of the kids at school, especially the younger ones, may have thought Jimmy was a scream, but some of the adults in town, especially those with ties to the older Vermont families that have always valued common sense more than cash, began to view Jimmy as a headache. People wondered why he always seemed to be zooming around the back roads in his car with Robert rather than studying or working, and there was a definite contingent that thought he was headed for trouble.

Robert Childs, one of Chelsea's elected "listors," who assess property for tax purposes, told *The Boston Globe*, "Jimmy Parker wasn't quite wild, but his parents were permissive, [and he's] shunned by a major population of the school.

"This does not surprise me in the least," continued Childs, who has two school-aged children himself. "These kids weren't coming home from a job after school. These kids were unsupervised and on the streets. They aren't pillars of the community."

"Jimmy's always been a spoiled brat," said John Upham, who ran a liquor and variety store in town. "He's arrogant. He's kind of a wise guy, I'd say. Just the way he carries himself," Upham told the *Rutland Herald*.

There was muttering around Upham's store and across the street at Button's feed shop that the Parkers needed to reign Jimmy in and pound some sense into him. However, to others in the village, the Parkers didn't seem like the kind of parents who were apt to raise a monster.

Far from being disengaged in the town, John and Joan Parker seemed involved in Jimmy's schooling and with the life of the village. John Parker coached the junior high basketball team for years before turning his attention to expanding the recreational area at the edge of the village.

"John is almost single-handedly responsible for building the new baseball fields in Chelsea. This guy was on the recreation committee, they raised the money, they got the site work donated by the local bulldozer guy, they mowed the grass with their own lawn mowers," said close family friend Kevin Ellis, a former reporter for *The Burlington Free Press* who has gone on to become a lobbyist with Bob Sherman in Montpelier.

John Parker built Ellis' house and was the organizing

force behind the Chelsea men's basketball team that the pair have played on together for years. "It's a central Vermont men's league, and John holds it all together for us here," Ellis said.

Ellis just knew Jimmy Parker as his friend's son, but he still saw him and spoke with him regularly. "I didn't see any signs," Ellis recalled. "I don't know what to think about this. Jimmy is a very bright, enterprising young man. I've seen him playing pick-up hockey in town, and pick-up basketball, and I know he's into music."

Jimmy was getting better and better at the bass guitar, and he had gone from piano lessons to an electric keyboard, and had thoughts of eventually becoming a professional musician.

When his long-time music teacher at Chelsea high school left during what was to have been the start of Parker's junior year, Jimmy transferred to Spaulding High School, a half-hour away in the nearby city of Barre, in order to be in a larger music program.

Spaulding students thought Jimmy was sort of funny, but weird, and he quickly decided that he wasn't enjoying being just another kid in a much larger student body. By December, he was headed back to Chelsea's high school, and although he wasn't going to be officially re-enrolled there until the spring 2001 term, he was sitting in on classes in the weeks before and after the murders.

For all of the examination and soul-searching that Chelsea did about Jimmy and Robert in the weeks and months following their arrests, the simple fact of the matter was that if it hadn't been for the devastating accusation leveled at them by Hanover Homicide Task Force, many in the community would have been perfectly happy writing off their excesses and faults as being within the bounds of small-town adolescent behavior.

The image most residents had of the pair in the days before the murders was from the May 2000 Chelsea Raft Race. When the winter snow starts to melt in the Green

Mountains, Vermont's little regional rivers start to swell. Around many small towns, the residents can be seen getting out whatever old junk can be scrounged from barns and dooryards to build rafts for their town's annual raft race. The purpose isn't to win, it's to laugh your ass off while you watch dozens of your friends try to stay out of the ice cold water as they drift through town in silly costumes on whatever contraption they have nailed, wired, taped, and stapled together out of old boards, feed bags, inner tubes, and beer kegs.

Rob and Jimmy took an early lead in the 2000 race, and even though one of their inner tubes sprung a leak, they sailed over the finish-line way ahead of the pack. Ever the clowns, Jimmy and Rob sank the raft as the crowd roared approval, and then splashed ashore.

Their win got them their picture in the local papers. Less than a year later, their pictures would be on the front pages of papers from coast to coast.

chapter 29

What few people in Chelsea knew before the teens were named as the suspects in the Zantop homicides was that they had already had one relatively substantial brush with the law.

Both Robert Tulloch and Jimmy Parker, and some of the other boys in their immediate circle of friends, had been put through a court-ordered "juvenile diversion" program designed to keep first-time offenders out of the regular criminal trial system in Vermont.

The cause had been a set of apparent break-ins in Chelsea during the summer of 2000 that had been largely explained away at the time as "a big misunderstanding."

"One person's break-in could be another person's adolescent hijinks," noted Parker family friend Kevin Ellis.

Robert, Jimmy, and several other friends had been in the habit of playing "ball tag," which, like it sounds, is a game of tag played by throwing a ball at the other players. The catch is that it's played indoors. It takes a particularly brave (or absent) parent to countenance the idea of a group of teenage boys running, ducking, and diving through a house while throwing a ball back and forth at each other down hallways, through doors, and around corners. Rob's big, spooky house was an ideal place to play the game, but after a while the group began appearing in other people's houses. That's where the story gets murky, because court records involving juveniles are kept secret.

There were two known incidents in which Rob and Jimmy and others were found in houses that they appeared to have entered without the owners' consent. One didn't result in the police being called; the other did.

The first incident occurred in April 2000 at the home of local glassblower Robin Mix, and his wife Susan Dollenmaier. Susan ran a large high-end fabric import business called Anachini out of the neighboring town of Tunbridge. The couple had twin 15-year-old daughters, Ivy and Tess Mix, who attended the Chelsea School and had invited Rob and Jimmy to stop by and see a movie.

Apparently when Rob, Jimmy, and two other local boys got to the house and found no one home, they discovered that one of the doors wasn't locked and just let themselves in. Robin Mix arrived home that evening to find the four of them in his basement watching a movie and cooking spaghetti.

"They didn't break in," Robin Mix told the *Valley News*. "They came in when nobody was home. In fact, they had been invited." Nonetheless, Mix didn't look happy, and when he asked if the boys were going to eat the food they said, "No, we better go," and hurriedly left.

Mix was on the brink of calling the boys' parents when he learned that his daughters had told the boys they could come over to watch a movie. Since nothing was disturbed, Mix decided to drop the issue. "It was very innocuous and they left a thank-you note," Dollenmaier later told *The Boston Globe*. "I didn't think much about it until this all happened."

The second incident, which resulted in the boys being sent through the court diversion program, took place later in the summer when a group of boys, including Parker and Tulloch, let themselves into the home of Julia Purcell, another one of their classmates at the Chelsea School, through an unlocked window.

The Purcells were on vacation at the time, and the boys reportedly played ball tag in the house as a "prank" for a period of time before leaving without apparently taking anything from the residence, which sits up on the Chelsea–Vershire town line.

The break-in was discovered by the home's owner, Diane Ward of Vershire, who was renting the property to Julia's mother Fran Purcell. Fran didn't want to press charges, but Diane insisted.

"At the time, it seemed so innocent, because they're such nice boys. You wonder if you should have blown the whistle then, but I couldn't believe there was anything beyond kids playing," Fran Purcell told the Associated Press, adding that at the time, it didn't strike her as a warning of things to come. "In retrospect, if they are guilty they should have been reprimanded strongly, but that's in retrospect," Purcell said.

It did strike the Orange County Sheriff's Department and the Vermont State Police as a warning sign. Both agencies questioned Tulloch and Parker in connection with a series of other unexplained break-ins around the region, but no other charges were filed.

Former Orange County Sheriff Sam Frank, who retired in the Fall of 2000 and moved to Virginia, would only say of Tulloch and Parker, "I dealt with them professionally." But others in law enforcement said that they felt strongly that Parker and Tulloch were involved in other "B&Es" around the county—they just couldn't prove it.

"There are some crimes when you know someone did it but you don't have the smoking gun," a law enforcement source told *The Boston Globe*, referring to the other incidents, after which authorities had a number of "heart to hearts" with Robert and Jimmy. But, the source continued, "there's some people . . . with an attitude problem and they don't care."

Investigators working on the Zantop murders would eventually question Julia Purcell, her mother, and the Mix family about the break-ins at their residences, and they spoke with several of the other boys who were involved, looking for what was termed "a pattern of behavior."

Whether or not there were more than just two incidents, the fact remained that nothing about the invasions at the

Purcell and Mix residences looked remotely like what had happened at the Zantops' home in Etna. Even in light of Tulloch and Parker's proclivity to enter other people's houses, the Zantop murders still looked much more like a premeditated attack than some sort of burglary attempt, let alone a game of ball tag, gone awry.

As investigators looking for any connection between the two Chelsea teens and the Zantops studied the summer 2000 break-ins, one remarkable coincidence did catch their attention.

Diane Ward, the landlady from Vershire who had discovered and ultimately pressed charges against Robert Tulloch and Jimmy Parker for the Purcell break-in, was the main home health care worker for ailing Dartmouth Professor Richard Stoiber in the last years of his life.

It was Dick Stoiber's birthday party that Half Zantop was supposed to have attended on the evening of the Saturday that he was killed. Diane Ward and her family were also friends with Arizona State University Professor Stanley Williams. In fact, it was Ward's nephew who had shot the moose and made the moose stew that Williams picked up the Monday following the murders.

Diane Ward knew Stanley Williams and Half Zantop because of her close association with Dick Stoiber. And she knew Tulloch and Parker because she had had them arrested. Ward's husband Steve, the Vershire assistant fire chief, owns a garage and tow truck service on the height of the land in Vershire, and it was Ward's Garage that the Vermont State Police had called to tow away the Parkers' cars in the middle of the night when they first executed the search warrants on the boys' homes.

Despite the ripple of excitement the overlapping connections with the Wards initially sent through the investigation, they didn't seem to mean anything useful. Ward didn't really know of the teens beyond the incident with them at her rental house, and she certainly had never had any reason to interact with them to the point that they would have learned about, let alone killed, the friend of a friend of hers in Hanover. After Vermont State Police detectives had a chance to talk with Diane Ward about the matter, it appeared to be just one of those six-degrees-of-separation coincidences that riddle regions as generally unpopulated as the Upper Connecticut River Valley.

Diane Ward was furious when the connection was picked up by the media and printed in newspapers across the Northeast, and broadcast on television. A few evenings later, one of the reporters who broke the story got her car stuck in a snow bank outside of Chelsea and called Ward's Garage for assistance. Diane recognized the name and headed out on the call with the tow truck. She read the reporter the riot act before yanking her car back onto the road.

chapter 30

By the time 2001 had rolled around, Rob Tulloch and Jimmy Parker had spent most of their free time hanging around with each other for the previous year. They had climbed rocks outdoors and rock walls indoors, hung out on the village green, played ball tag through their houses, teased girls, kicked hackey sacks, and cruised the back roads of Orange County together for countless hours. But at 4 A.M. on the morning of Monday, February 19, half a nation away in central Indiana, their shared interests and their very destinies were about to abruptly part company, quite possibly for the rest of their lives.

Stuck in the Henry County Jail, a twenty-year-old facility that authorities there like to point out is still "very clean," both of the boys had the distinction of being considered juveniles under Indiana law, which pegs an adult as being 18 or older. But once they returned to New Hampshire, which draws the line at 17, the slight split in the boys' ages was going to amount to a night-and-day difference in their circumstances.

As New Hampshire State Police Sergeants Robert Bruno and Russ Conte boarded flights to Indiana along with Assistant Attorney General Kelly Ayotte and others, the boys' parents and friends were also rushing to get out to the center of the country to see what was going on.

Attorney Dennis Brown, a college friend of John Parker, flew from San Diego to Indiana to help represent the two boys. The Chelsea-based lobbyist Kevin Ellis, John Parker's long-time friend, also flew out from Vermont to help the family.

Ellis went to work trying to counter rumors that were circulating about the boys, including the notion that John Parker had given them some sort of head start after he found Jimmy's note, and another which said that Robert's girlfriend Christiana Usenza had once worked as a housecleaner for the Zantops and had been having an affair with Half, thereby driving Robert into a jealous killing rage. Both notions were preposterous, Ellis insisted. Far from encouraging Jimmy to run from authorities, the Parkers were in fact relieved that he was somewhere safe where they could work on his defense, Ellis explained. "They're pleased that their son is in custody so they can get him back home," Ellis told reporters.

The rumors had been circulating around the Upper Valley as people tried to connect the dots and imagine ways in which the teens could have come into contact with the Zantops. In particular, Ellis singled out the rumor, which had never been an official theory, that Christiana had cleaned the Zantops' house. Ellis made a point of telling reporters that Christiana had never worked as a house cleaner, not for the Zantops nor for anyone else, and neither had her mother.

Suddenly the Henry County Jail became the center of the Zantop investigation, as lawyers met with both boys early in the day and told them that family members would be flying out from Vermont to see them.

While at the jail, the boys, who were, after all, the focus of a nationwide search conducted by the FBI, had a certain celebrity attached to their care, and although they were much too wrapped up in their own concerns to notice it, much of their stay there was personally supervised by Henry County High Sheriff Kim Cronk.

The boys had been searched, their street clothes had been taken away, and both were now dressed in the kind of black-and-white-striped prison uniforms that are most familiar from cartoon caricatures of burglars. In Indiana, the black-and-white outfits are issued to inmates who aren't allowed to leave the prison. Blue-and-white outfits go to "trustees"—those prisoners who are trusted with special privileges in the jails—and green-and-white outfits are worn by prisoners who can leave for work release programs during the day.

Police wanted the two teens kept largely separate from each other, and from the rest of the prison population. A mattress was shoved into the prison weight room, and Tulloch was left in there with a box of Kleenex that he used up crying as the morning progressed. A mattress for Parker was pushed into the interview room, and he lay on it with a blanket over his head as his lawyers tracked in and out to ask questions.

While at the jail, the boys were allowed to meet with their parents in their own cells rather than in the common visiting area. Cronk said that wasn't as much a humanitarian gesture, as simply an acknowledgment of the fact that they were considered juveniles in Indiana. "That wasn't unusual given their ages," he said.

Michael and Diane Tulloch arrived a short time later and met with Robert. Afterwards Diane told reporters gathered outside the facility, "We love our son, and we want the press to know that he's innocent until proven guilty." Late Monday evening, John and Joan Parker arrived at the jail in New Castle and met with Jimmy for an emotional half-hour.

The tension of the cross-country flight from authorities, their capture, and the sudden arrival of their parents were tearing at both teens, and the boys spent much of Tuesday morning, February 20, crying in their cells.

"They were not put into the main area," Cronk explained. "They were kept in some of the smaller cells in our observation area." Those cells had a one-way window where authorities could look in and see what was going on. "Because of the double murder charges we had to put on extra staffing to watch them at night," Cronk said.

Mid-day, the pair were perp-walked, with a sheriff on

each arm, a block and a half through downtown New Castle to the Henry County Superior Court. Television crews, newspaper photographers, and reporters watching the teens' every move made it a small parade as the boys winced their way in chains and flip-flops up the courthouse steps and into the hearing room before Judge Michael Peyton.

Tulloch went in first, wearing the clothes he had been captured in, a black sweater with a faint brown bird's-eye pattern knit through it, and blue jeans.

Tulloch stood before the judge with red-rimmed eyes and had little to say other than his name throughout the brief appearance. With his father seated behind him, he spent much of his time biting his upper lip, looking very much as though he was going to start crying again at any moment.

On the advice of Edward Dunsmore, his Indiana attorney, Tulloch signed the papers waiving his right to contest his extradition back to New Hampshire to face murder charges. His hand trembled noticeably as he did so.

When it was Parker's turn before Judge Peyton, his attorney Richard Kammen said that the teen wasn't ready to waive nor to contest his extradition, so another hearing was set for Parker on the following Tuesday. Parker kept his eyes down during most of his appearance and answered just "yes" and "no" to a series of short questions from the judge. Afterwards, Kammen told reporters that Parker's parents had skipped the hearing because of the large media contingent that was covering it. "Jim is a 16-year-old, and obviously he is somewhat shell-shocked about the situation, and he and his family are trying to come to grips with things," Kammen told the *Valley News*.

The next morning, Wednesday, February 21, the FBI sent a small corporate jet piloted by two agents to Indiana to retrieve Tulloch and return him to the Granite State.

Dressed back in his own street clothes, Tulloch was bundled on to the jet without much ceremony and handcuffed to a seat inside.

Facing multiple charges that carry a maximum sentence of life without parole in New Hampshire, Rob Tulloch must have realized that the ninety-minute flight had the potential to be the last journey of any significant distance the would-be world traveler would ever take.

Touching down at 2:37 P.M. at the Lebanon Municipal Airport amidst the snow-shrouded hills overlooking the Connecticut River, Tulloch was met by a veritable who's-who of the Zantop investigation. When he stepped out onto the tarmac dragging waist and ankle chains, the reception he got was every bit as frosty as the outside air on that still New Hampshire afternoon. Grim-faced troopers from the state police and police officers from Hanover in full uniform each grabbed an arm, and Tulloch was led shuffling to a waiting motorcade of cruisers as Major Barry Hunter and other detectives walked alongside, saying nothing. The message was clear—they had worked round the clock for nearly a month under intense public scrutiny, and they were returning to town with their suspect.

In the convoy of police cars, Tulloch was driven rapidly back to the Hanover Police Station, where he was once again fingerprinted and formally arrested on New Hampshire soil for the double murder. Police officers and staff who couldn't see into the small booking area crowded into the dispatch center at the front of the building to watch on closed-circuit television as Tulloch went through the brief process. They had spent a month wondering and searching for their suspects. This was the first chance many of those who had put in long nights on the case had to get a good look at him.

Tulloch was then bundled back into a cruiser for the short ride through Hanover to the new Lebanon District Courthouse up on a hill by the Dartmouth–Hitchcock Medical Center.

In New Hampshire, the district courts cannot take pleas in felony cases, they must await a grand jury indictment before the case is handed over to the county superior court that has jurisdiction. Thus, when Tulloch came in for his arraignment, the process involved only the judge reading him the charges and making sure he understood them before setting bail or other conditions of release, if appropriate.

As reporters packed the lobby outside the courtroom door, Tulloch was led into the brightly lit modern white courtroom at 6 P.M.

Wearing cuffs, a waist chain, and leg shackles, with his now slightly blonde-tinged hair mussed up at an odd angle, he looked pained, and kept his eyes on the floor as two uniformed officers once again marshaled him around by the arms and planted him behind the defense table. His parents, looking strained, sat a short distance away in the front row ahead of sixty reporters, a throng of onlookers, and an array of detectives and prosecutors from the case who had packed into the jury box to get a clearer look at the proceedings.

"Do you understand the crimes with which you have been charged?" asked District Court Judge Albert J. Cirone, Jr.

"Yes, Your Honor," Tulloch replied with a slight nod of his head.

That was it. Cirone ordered Tulloch held without bail until further notice. The hearing had taken less than ten minutes and Tulloch was headed out the back door to a police cruiser for the ride to the Grafton County Correctional Center in North Haverhill, New Hampshire.

As he stepped out the back door surrounded by police, downcast and dragging his feet, a voice in the waiting crowd of cameramen who were stacked shoulder-to-shoulder for the shot shouted out to Tulloch. "Rob! It's DeRoss! I'm here for you, man!" yelled his former sixth-grade teacher DeRoss Kellogg.

Tulloch perked up, faced into the bright quartz lights of the television cameras, and said in a firm, clear voice, "Thanks, DeRoss. My parents said you were in the courtroom, and I really appreciate it." With that, he was put into the back seat of the waiting cruiser.

Back in Indiana, Parker was still locked up in Henry County while his family and his lawyers considered their options. Breakfast was usually cereal and donuts, lunch was a hot meal like beef with noodles, vegetables, and fruit punch while dinner consisted of basics like bologna sandwiches. "They are very common meals," Cronk noted. But because of his juvenile status, Parker was allowed to order in chips, Nutri-Grain bars, and a few Cokes. He was also allowed to meet frequently and relatively freely with his parents.

John Parker shot hoops in the prison gymnasium with Jimmy. Joan came in and spoke with him and hugged him. During the bulk of the day, when he was locked up in his segregated eight-foot–by–eight-foot cell, Jimmy played solitaire or read a paperback science fiction book called *Rama II* that he had picked out of the prison library.

Corrections officers described Parker as polite, and said he hardly spoke to them. During one of his rare conversations, Parker asked Henry County Sheriff Kim Cronk what the town of New Castle was like and how large it was. Cronk told him the town had just 18,000 residents, but Parker, from a town less than a tenth that size, didn't think it sounded that small. "He's in a strange environment. I told him it's a small community, but I guess it's bigger than his," Cronk told the *Boston Herald*.

While this was going on, the FBI was back in Henry County Superior Court asking officials to seal the video surveillance tapes of the two teenagers inside their jail cells that were taken during their first two days together at the facility. New Hampshire authorities wanted to look at the tapes, which didn't include audio, to see if anything had transpired that they could use as evidence. The judge granted the request, and the tapes were forwarded to investigators.

By Friday, Parker's lawyers had made the decision not

to contest the extradition back to New Hampshire to face
the charges, and Parker was walked back over to the courthouse to sign the papers waiving his rights to contest his
return. He met with his parents privately for an hour before
appearing again before the judge and signing the paperwork.

Afterwards, on the steps of the courthouse, John Parker,
with his long-time friend Dennis Brown by his side, turned
to reporters and said simply, "I can't believe that Jimmy
was capable of committing this crime."

Jimmy Parker had walked over to the courthouse wearing a stiff blue jail-issue denim jacket over his prison uniform, but on the way back he decided to forgo it. "It was
nice out," he explained to Sheriff Cronk when he returned
to the lockup.

Parker would spend his fifth and final night in Indiana
at the Henry County Jail. On Saturday, the same FBI
Cessna Citation V jet that had flown Tulloch to New Hampshire three days earlier touched down again at the airfield
to pick up Parker. On-board was Hanover Police Chief
Nick Giaccone, who would accompany Parker back to New
Hampshire. After Parker boarded, authorities also loaded
three cardboard boxes onto the jet containing both boys'
as-yet unopened backpacks and the other loose items that
were with them when they were arrested.

The boxes were mostly stuffed with clothing. It seemed
like each boy must have scooped up an armload of it before
they fled on Friday night. In addition to whatever was inside the backpacks, Tulloch and Parker had been wearing
long johns, long pants with military "battle dress uniform"–
style tan pants over them, underwear shirts, shirts, sweaters,
jackets, and coats when they were captured. Police also
seized a nickel and five nails that they found in the boys'
pockets, a plastic bottle of water, and a blue nylon wallet
containing $92 in US currency.

As the jet sailed in above the snowy hills that rise on
both sides of the Connecticut River, a white-and-blue Han-

over Police cruiser was parked prominently out on the tarmac in front of three dark green New Hampshire State Police cruisers waiting for the plane to taxi into position.

With swift precision, the FBI pilots pulled the jet up to the North Ramp of the Lebanon Municipal Airport just before 3 P.M., and cut the engines.

Parker looked tired and defeated as the door popped open and he worked his way gingerly down the small ladder in his handcuffs and leg chains. Once again, Hanover police officers and state police troopers joined detectives in a slow march with Parker to the waiting cruisers, as photographers shot the scene through telephoto lenses from a balcony on the upper deck of a nearby aviation company building.

Dressed in a blue pullover shirt, bright blue athletic pants with yellow stripes, and new sneakers, Parker barely looked around at the waiting swarm of police, troopers, and investigators who had shown up to escort him back to the Hanover Police Station for processing.

Unlike Tulloch, this was to be Parker's last public appearance for the rest of the year. As a juvenile, his hearings would be closed to the public and the press, and if he could hang onto his juvenile status and avoid being tried as an adult, even with a conviction and a maximum sentence, he would have to be released by the state when he hit his twenty-first birthday.

Prosecutors immediately filed paperwork to have Parker "certified" as an adult, but his attorneys settled in to fight the process tooth and nail. In their few public statements about Parker, his court-appointed attorneys took pains always to refer to him as "a boy" and "a child."

Unlike Tulloch, who was now sitting in an isolation cell under twenty-three-hour-a-day lockdown in the maximum security unit of the decrepit Grafton County Correctional Center, Parker was whisked off to the new high-security juvenile detention facility on the old state hospital grounds in Concord, where conditions and privileges were much,

much better. It would be a short-lived reprieve. On May 24, Parker's seventeenth birthday arrived, and he was automatically transferred to an adult facility in Belknap County in the northern part of New Hampshire. Officials didn't want to take any chances that the pair could come into contact with each other before their trials.

chapter 31

Two days after Tulloch and Parker were captured in Indiana, and just five days after the initial article ran, *The Boston Globe* did an about-face on their front page story pegging the motive for the double murder to an affair that Half Zantop was supposedly having.

Dartmouth Professor Alexis Jetter had been infuriated by the article, and had called *Washington Post* media critic and columnist Howard Kurtz to denounce both the original piece and what she saw as the *Globe*'s failure to retract it in light of the arrest of the two teens.

Kurtz had in turn called the *Globe*'s editor, Matthew V. Storin, and questioned the paper's actions for a column he was preparing about the story that would run that Thursday.

Storin beat Kurtz to the punch and on Wednesday, February 21, the *Boston Globe* ran a "To Our Readers" note on its front page, saying that three law enforcement sources involved in the investigation had been the source of the affair allegation.

Storin continued, "In the days since the story appeared, the *Globe* has held several additional discussions with its original sources. The sources said the information they supplied was correct to the best of their knowledge at the time it was provided. However, in light of the current focus on teenage suspects Robert W. Tulloch and James J. Parker, the sources now concede that the extramarital affair theory is not correct."

Storin concluded by saying that the *Globe* was simply trying to provide complete information on the case from officials they believed to be reliable sources and that the paper regretted the pain the affair story had "undoubtedly" caused the Zantop family and community.

The next day, Kurtz's column ran in the *Washington Post*, noting that in an interview Tuesday morning, Storin had defended the story. "We had three very good sources," Storin told Kurtz. "The only thing worse than being wrong in the first place is saying you were wrong when you were right."

In his column, Kurtz quoted Alexis Jetter denouncing the *Globe* piece as a "sick, perverse, headline-grabbing story. The coverage was scurrilous. It was desperate. It was the lowest form of journalism. They were trying to play catch-up on a story they were way behind on, and they took a risk on a bad piece of information," Jetter told Kurtz.

Whatever the *Globe* and its critics might have had to say about the matter, in the absence of any other official explanation of a motive, or indeed, any form of connection between the Zantops and the two kids from Chelsea, the affair theory would continue to hold center stage in the minds of many members of the public who were following the case. Without anything else concrete to go on, the notion that the killings boiled down to a crime of passion on someone's part would continue to thrive in dozens of different permutations around the water coolers and diner counters of the Upper Valley.

chapter 32

The notion that there had to be a connection between whoever killed the Zantops and the Zantops themselves had haunted the investigation from its first day.

So much about the killing looked targeted and not random, motivated, not motiveless, yet even with two suspects in custody, police were clearly having a difficult time finding any convincing link between the victims and their accused murderers.

At the request of investigators, Dartmouth College quietly began poring through its computers and records looking for any reference to Tulloch or Parker. They looked for any evidence that they had taken a course or attended an event or done something somewhere that would have brought them into contact with Dartmouth, and maybe even the Zantops. After days spent checking, nothing turned up, not a whisper.

Early on in the investigation, it was noticed that the day the Zantops were killed, January 27, also happened to be Holocaust Remembrance Day in Israel and parts of Europe.

Asked whether the date was a coincidence or a significant clue, Assistant Attorney General Kelly Ayotte said, "With respect to the fact that they were murdered on the Holocaust Remembrance Day . . . in terms of the investigation itself, that's information that we would consider, and we haven't ruled that out."

It's a date that doesn't formally appear on many American calendars, but it commemorates the day that Soviet troops arrived to liberate the survivors of the Auschwitz concentration camp.

The Zantops were certainly German, but they weren't Jewish, and while they had strong opinions about the need to preserve individual rights and help prisoners of conscience around the world, it was hard to see where anything they had said or done along those lines would have provided any impetus for their murders.

The Zantops' personal and professional views were diametrically opposed to Nazism, but it was hard to imagine them being anywhere near the top of even the most hypothetical Neo-Nazi "hit list."

Then, on the evening of Thursday, February 22, while Chelsea residents were gathering at their church on the North Common for the "town meeting" discussion of how to handle the boys' arrests, ABC's *Primetime Thursday* television magazine aired a report saying that the investigators who'd spent thirty-six hours combing through the Tulloch household had come up with Neo-Nazi Holocaust revisionism and white supremacist literature in Robert's bedroom.

The investigators had indeed spent a considerable time going through the Tullochs' house; they even went back to the courts twice on that Saturday to get additional search warrants allowing them to seize items that they had noticed during their initial search, including the boy's computer. One of the other supplemental search warrants made mention of the red copy of *Der Fuerher* on Rob's bookshelf, the supposedly violent video games, and another book that made mention of the Ku Klux Klan. However, after the ABC report aired, detectives took the unusual step of taking some reporters aside and assuring them that was "not a direction the investigation is going in."

Friends of Tulloch's also expressed immediate doubts about the report. They remembered seeing dozens of history books on World War II in Rob's room, including *The Rise and Fall of the Third Reich* and Adolf Hitler's rambling *Mein Kampf*, but these were just a few of the wide range of books that the teen read voraciously in his spare time.

There was nothing there that anyone remembered as being any more subversive than Albert Camus' *The Stranger*.

Taken as a whole, the Northeast is one of the more liberal regions of the country, and Vermont, despite its overwhelming white Anglo-Saxon population, is especially known for its tolerance of quirky neighbors, divergent viewpoints, alternate lifestyles, and minority rights. While New Hampshire's license plates say "Live free or die," Vermont's could just as easily read "Live and let live."

There was one major state-wide controversy in 2000 and 2001 that swept through Vermont when the state's supreme court ruled that a close reading of the Vermont Constitution made it clear that same-sex couples who wanted to marry had to be given the same rights and benefits under state law that heterosexual married couples enjoy. This issue essentially split the state down the middle, half for and half against, and it caused a debate that was wrenching to watch in communities that normally liked to concentrate on what they agreed on, rather than on where they differed. The subsequent decision by the state's legislature to grant gay and lesbian couples the right to enter into "civil unions," which were marriages in all but name, sparked a significant backlash.

The epicenter of that backlash was the section of Orange County that included Chelsea, but even there, it was far from a homogenous opposition. The symbol of the anti–civil unions movement was a series of plain white signs with black letters that began cropping up on barns and trailers, and even trees throughout the region saying simply, "Take Back Vermont."

Tourists that fall mistook the "Take Back Vermont" signs as an exhortation to buy more maple syrup, but Vermonters of all stripes knew instantly that those three words were a not-so-subtle jibe from the "Real Vermonters," who lived and died by traditional values handed down by generation after generation of largely agricultural families, at the "Flatlanders," who had spent much of the last forty years flooding into Vermont and replacing farms with up-scale condos and putting cute little coffee shops in place of corner diners.

Still, even most of the heated debates about the issue that took place in Vermont were downright cordial compared to the venom that came in from over the state lines during the weeks leading up to the Legislature's decision. When a group of evangelical Christians from the middle of Kansas showed up one morning on the granite steps of Vermont's little Capitol Building in Montpelier with signs saying "God Hates Fags" and "Gays Burn in Hell," even many of the most outspoken local critics of civil unions felt obliged to take time out from the debate to clarify that they weren't suggesting same-sex couples shouldn't be part of the community. Several took pains to assure reporters that, if called, they would still show up at their gay neighbors' residences with jumper cables in the middle of the winter without a moment's hesitation.

During the debate, the Zantops had sent several emails to friends in Vermont encouraging them to support the civil unions movement, but nobody particularly remembered Rob or Jimmy caring one way or the other. In fact, if anything, Rob's friends would describe his political views as liberal.

They certainly didn't remember either teen expressing any bent towards Neo-Nazi or Ku Klux Klan–like organizations.

Asked if she thought the pair could ever be involved with a hate group, Christiana Usenza was adamant. "Not at all. They are not prejudiced in any way that I know of," she said.

Other friends agreed, dismissing out of hand any notion of either the Tulloch or Parker families being involved in any sort of anti-Semitism or other hate group activities.

Just over a week later, when the Neo-Nazi angle was still in play in some quarters, Attorney General Philip

McLaughlin issued one of his rare flat-out denials, and said that *Primetime Thursday* had gotten it wrong. "It was inaccurate," McLaughlin said. "I have no idea what it was that they based that report on."

chapter 33

The investigators searching for a connection that would provide a logical link between the Zantops and the two teens spent a lot of time looking at the issue of rock climbing.

Off the cuff, it seemed like the fact that Half was a geology professor, which had to do with rocks, coupled with the fact that Rob and Jimmy were avid climbers, which had to with rocks, might somehow have connected the three.

Reality was much murkier.

Half had been a serious rock climber when he was much younger. He had climbed the Pyrenees and the Alps with his father and older brother when he was a boy growing up in Spain and Germany. In his twenties, he had picked up the sport in the Western United States and Canada when he attended the University of Washington.

"He was one of the best. I say that because we did some of the hardest routes and first ascents around the mountains, and you only did that with the best climbers," said Alex Bertulis, a Seattle architect who met Half Zantop as an undergraduate student at Washington State University in the early 1960s, to *The Boston Globe*.

"We did a 10-day traverse of the Picket Range and did some awesome climbing, and made some first ascents," Bertulis recalled in the *Globe* interview. "One of the most epic achievements was a 2,000-foot vertical descent of the north face of Mount Terror, which was aptly named." That accomplishment won the pair a mention in *The American Alpine Journal* in 1965.

In 1965, Half also climbed the 10,880-foot Unicorn Peak in Yosemite National Park. He ascended right up the direct north face of the peak. But it was an accident shortly thereafter on Echo Peak at Yosemite that convinced Half he was pushing his luck. Half took a fall on a vertical rock face when he was leading Bertulis towards the top, and he broke his ankle. Hobbling on the long hike back to the car, Half realized that the plunge could just as easily have killed him. He decided to quit climbing and focus on getting his Ph.D.

Half stayed interested in climbing, and would occasionally stop by the indoor climbing wall at the River Valley Club in Hanover, a gym where he and Susanne had memberships, to watch people climb it. Even more rarely, he would talk about his exploits as a younger man with people who were particularly interested in technical climbing, but it was not something he was actively interested in, in the years before his death.

The Hanover Police Department raised the idea of a possible rock climbing connection when they sent out a blanket email to all the members of the Dartmouth Outing Club asking if any of them had bought or sold any equipment in dealings with local residents between December 15, 2000, and the present. "The information about equipment sales may shed more light on the ongoing Zantop investigation," wrote Hanover Police Detective Eric Bates in the email. A member of the Outing Club later told reporters that a check of their records hadn't found any such sales during the time period Bates asked about.

Rob Tulloch and Jimmy Parker didn't own a lot of equipment, just a practice board and a harness, so when they went climbing in the summer, oftentimes with Christiana Usenza and other friends, it was more on the order of "bouldering" or scrambling up small rock formations in Chelsea and the neighboring towns around the Green Mountains.

"They weren't professionals. They were just learning," Usenza explained.

Throughout the year, Rob and Jimmy had also plunked down $50 a month for memberships at Petra Cliffs in Burlington. They spent four or five hours at a time there using their indoor rock wall two or three times each week. They were well liked by the staff, and considered upper-intermediate climbers at the facility.

Tulloch and Parker also visited other indoor rock walls around the state, and on one occasion, on October 3, 2000, they stopped in and paid $15 for a one-day pass to use the thirty-foot climbing wall at the River Valley Club in Hanover. They lied about their ages, saying that they were 18 at the time.

Friends of the Zantops dismissed the possible connection, saying that Half never used the rock wall at the club, and club records confirmed that he had never signed up to climb. A check of the club records also showed that neither of the Zantops were at the club at any time on October 3, nor on the day before, nor the day after.

Another potential connection that looked promising at first, but which evaporated once authorities investigated further, was the coincidence of the Zantops' and the Parkers' summer 2000 vacations in Maine.

The Zantops had rented their usual cabin at the Hiram Blake Camp from July 15 to August 5, 2000. The day after the Zantops' left, the Parkers went to stay at the summer home of Ned Battey, father of Jimmy's classmate and friend Kip Battey, in nearby Brookville, Maine.

New Hampshire State Troopers went and talked to people in both summer communities, but could not find any way in which the Zantops' and the Parkers' stays in the area overlapped, given the divergent dates and the fact that the Zantops had returned promptly to Hanover at the end of the three-week vacation.

Another question that faced investigators trying to figure out whatever logic might underlie the Zantops' deaths, was how to account for Tulloch and Parker's movements on the day before, the day of, and the day after the murders.

Townspeople recalled that Parker's parents were on a cycling vacation that had taken them from Savannah, Georgia, to Charlestown, West Virginia, the weekend of the murders, but close friends hadn't seen Rob or Jimmy around that weekend at all.

Rob had reappeared in school on Monday with his odd knee injury and the weird story about the maple syrup tap that nobody was really buying.

"We all thought whatever it was that caused the leg injury, it certainly wasn't what he was telling us," recalled John O'Brien. "I joked about that when I talked to him on the phone. I was like 'Come on, Robert, this is the lamest excuse I've ever heard,' and that was about it."

Police had reported finding evidence of "surveillance of a building" amongst the writings seized from Robert's bedroom, and separate witnesses had reported seeing a green car at the Zantop residence that Friday, the day before the murders, and on the Saturday the murders took place.

Parker's mother's car, the one in which police found the bloodstained front passenger-side carpet, was a green 1996 Subaru station wagon.

Around 2:30 P.M. on Friday, January 26, Paul Newcity, a 40-year-old resident of nearby Canaan, New Hampshire, was riding east on Trescott Road with a friend when a dark green station wagon shot partway out from the Zantops' driveway and onto the road in front of him.

Newcity told Hanover Police Detective Eric Bates that the station wagon's young, male driver put nearly a fourth of the vehicle out into the roadway before stopping to allow him to pass. "That was definitely the house. It made a pretty strong impression on me. It was leaving fast. That's very out of the ordinary for the neighborhood," said Newcity in an interview with the *Valley News*. "People around there don't leave their yard at that rate of speed."

The green station wagon's sudden appearance forced

Newcity to swerve to avoid an accident. It happened so fast that Newcity wasn't sure whether there was more than one person in the other car, but he told Hanover police that he did get a quick look at the driver, who struck him as being a clean-shaven, thin white male in his twenties with dark hair. "It was all a flash, mostly," Newcity said.

On the Saturday the murders took place, the Mc-Collums' housecleaner saw a strange car pull into the McCollums' driveway, but authorities did not release details of that particular sighting.

There was somewhere Rob Tulloch was supposed to have been that Saturday, and he was missed.

Two nights before, on the evening of Thursday, January 25, Rob's close friend Kip Battey had called him and asked him to be his debate partner on Saturday at the annual tournament that was held at Hartford High School. If Rob didn't show, Kip, a varsity debater, would have to enter the match paired with a novice, and he thought that would hurt his chances of winning. Rob agreed to participate, and said he would meet him at the high school in White River Junction on Saturday morning.

When Rob didn't show up at Hartford High School at 8:30 A.M. on January 27 to register for the day's tournament, Battey was annoyed, but, he figured, "it was typical Robert," and didn't think much more about the matter. Battey went through several morning and afternoon rounds, and left with the rest of the students around 4 P.M. without ever having seen or heard a thing from Tulloch.

chapter 34

As the pursuit phase of the Zantop case slammed to a conclusion with the capture of the boys in Indiana, the prosecutorial phase began to gear up. Legal motions would begin flying fast and furious between court-appointed attorneys in New Hampshire and the attorney general's office as they prepared to present both cases to a grand jury for indictments, to petition the court to try Parker as an adult, and to ready Tulloch for trial on the charges early in 2002.

But for Robert Tulloch, time would come to a crashing halt after a long day spent on an FBI plane and the subsequent shuttling back and forth between the Hanover Police Station and the Lebanon District Court. That evening, while Parker still waited in the relative comfort of the Indiana jail pending his transfer to the Youth Detention Services Unit in Concord, Tulloch went straight into one of the maximum security units at the Grafton County Correctional Center in North Haverhill.

Situated in the middle of nowhere at the Grafton County Complex, the GCCC is a nondescript brick building with a peaked roof that you could almost miss as you drove along Route 10 past the neighboring courthouse and the Grafton County Nursing Home out front. Behind the prison is the prison farm, which looks much like any other farm except for the razor wire bordering the fields. The view out the windows is a postcard shot of the Vermont skyline, rolling cornfields with the Connecticut River winding between them and a round barn with black-and-white Holstein cows wandering the fields in front of the rising rows of low mountains. If there wasn't a correctional center sitting on it, the whole thing would be prime property.

Inside the aging building, the GCCC is most charitably described by former inmates as "a pit." Because the jail is tucked up in a forgotten corner of New Hampshire, there are few of the gang troubles and other hardcore problems that plague larger prisons in neighboring states. But at the same time, there is almost nothing to do, and very little in the way of amenities.

There are four maximum security blocks in the prison, and each block is usually home to between eight and twelve prisoners, depending on the population at the time.

Because he was checked in on a "pre-sentencing" basis for a violent crime, Tulloch was automatically lodged in the maximum security unit while he awaited his trial.

"The cells in max in Haverhill are really small," said a former inmate. "I could stand on the bottom bunk and put a hand on each wall and pull myself up to the top bunk."

Each max cell has a concrete floor, a combined toilet and a sink, two bunks, and an iron barred door with another solid door just outside that is closed at night and opened in the morning.

Immediately outside the door is a two-and-a-half-foot-wide metal catwalk that runs the length of the cell block.

Each of the prisoners in max is issued a single dark blue jumpsuit, two towels, and two pairs of underwear. If they have their own shoes, prisoners are allowed to wear them, but if they show up with boots or don't have their own footwear, they are given prison-issue sneakers, which the former inmate described as looking like "something they wore on *The Brady Bunch*."

Prisoners at Haverhill are only allowed to keep their issued items and pen and paper in their cells. They can check books and puzzles out of the prison library, but the only games allowed are cards.

The maximum security areas are always under twenty-three-hour-a-day-lock-down, but prisoners are allowed out into the yard once a day for an hour as a group, one cell block at a time; however, in the winter months very few prisoners actually venture outdoors. "It's pretty much everybody sitting around for an hour watching more television," the former inmate said.

There are pots of hot water in the main blocks that the prisoners can reach through the bars to make coffee or the Ramen Cup of Noodles soup that they can purchase from the prison commissary during their weekly trip to that small store.

The prisoners in Grafton County's maximum security units aren't allowed to work in the prison shops, and even those minimum security prisoners that do work don't earn any money. Cash is considered contraband at the jail and is forbidden, but each inmate does have an account, and if they or their families deposit money in it, they can use that money at the commissary to make purchases.

"They have a real short commissary list in Haverhill," says the former inmate. "You can purchase some things that they don't give you, like soap and shampoo and playing cards, and they have stuff like crackers, Ramen cup-of-noodles, instant coffee, cream and sugar packets, Kool-Aid, and honey buns. They've also got some candy like Skittles and chocolate bars that you can buy."

Meals come in the form of leftovers from the nearby state-run nursing home. Whatever the nursing home is eating, the prisoners are eating too. "You have to eat off a tray, and you get one scoop of everything. If you are hungry, you have to get it off somebody else who isn't eating all theirs," the former inmate says.

The jail does have cable TV channels, and there is a VCR linked to each cell block's TV system that the guards control. Individual prisoners can pay to rent movies, and by flipping a switch, all the prisoners in the same block can watch the same tape once the guard starts playing it. "New movies are three dollars and the old ones are ninety-nine cents," reports the former inmate.

Mail is distributed six days a week in the early afternoon

and prisoners can receive magazines that they or their friends and family have subscribed to, but they have to come from that publication or from a store, they can't be sent directly to them by individuals.

Despite the dismal conditions in the "very old buildings" at Grafton County Correctional and the limited amenities, the former inmate said that the one nice thing about it, compared to other prisons he had stayed at, was the relative lack of a hostile environment.

Tulloch's former sixth-grade teacher DeRoss Kellogg spent an hour visiting Rob, along with Tulloch's younger brother Kienan and Nancy Kerwin, the librarian at the Chelsea Public School, one afternoon shortly after his indictment. Kellogg later told *The Boston Globe* that it looked to him like Tulloch was doing well behind bars. "He seems to be living from week to week," said Kellogg. "He's not looking too far into the future. He's living in the present."

The trio spent most of the hour talking about books, especially the Ayn Rand books he had been reading in jail. "We talked a lot about *The Fountainhead* and *Atlas Shrugged*," Kellogg said.

No one brought up the murder case, but Tulloch made it a point to ask his younger brother about his grades. "Robert is still playing the older brother here," Kellogg told the *Globe*. "He was very insistent he found out how Kienan did on his latest report card."

Less than a month later, in mid-March, Larry Kumpf, a 41-year-old former heroin-dealing biker with a prison record as thick as a phone book, spent the better part of an evening in the cell block with Tulloch and got a much harsher view of the teen's life on the inside.

Kumpf had destroyed his liver with drugs during his wilder days, and between a couple of extremely close brushes with death, and having to live with dialysis, he has worked hard to turn his life around.

Now a frequent speaker at prisons across New England on behalf of Narcotics Anonymous, and a volunteer member of a court diversion and reparations board in Vermont, Kumpf had a rude awakening one afternoon in March. He was in the middle of a nap when police officers knocked on his apartment door and arrested him on an old fugitive warrant out of New Jersey that had just resurfaced.

While Kumpf worked to convince authorities that this was a big misunderstanding, which it turned out largely to be, he was lodged for the evening at the GCCC. Because of his extensive past record, and because guards figured he was probably not going to be staying long at the facility, Kumpf was put in the small max unit just inside the door from the guard station. Standing against a nearby wall trying to see the television outside, was a quiet, scared Robert Tulloch, wearing only a pair of blue prison pants and no shirt.

"I was locked down with him in max for about six or eight hours until I got bailed," Kumpf recalled. "He was real timid. It seemed that he was compliant to other prisoners and very frightened. There were jail guys that were pushing him around and he didn't know how to handle it. He didn't even know how to get a chair for himself. There were five of us in max at the time, and then there was a drunk they were trying to find a cell for that they just threw on one of the cots. He was just passed out the whole time I was there."

Kumpf remembered a small Puerto Rican fugitive from Massachusetts, covered in tattoos, who was sharing Tulloch's cell and seemed to have the upper hand over the 17-year-old and all the others in the twenty-foot-long cell block.

"This guy was sitting on all four chairs so he could see the TV better outside the max cells," Kumpf said. "I came along, and I'm kinda familiar with how this works, and I said, 'You've got four chairs there,' and the guy says, 'Yeah,' and I said, 'Well, one of them's mine. Give it up,' and he did," Kumpf laughed.

"I looked at Tulloch and I said, 'How long you been

standing there?' and he said, '21 days,' " Kumpf continued.

"Tulloch had pretty good black-and-blue marks on his back. We didn't talk about that, but I've seen that before and I knew what was going on," Kumpf said.

Kumpf felt sorry for Tulloch, and decided to get him one of the plastic stacking lawn chairs so he could sit and watch the television.

"I said, 'Well, look, you've got two bologna sandwiches there.' I said, 'Why don't you trade one of your sandwiches for a chair?' and he said, 'Okay,' and I went right up with him to the guy, and I said, 'Make sure you tell him that's a trade-off for the chair for good, not each day,' " Kumpf recalled.

"Tulloch didn't say nothing. He just looked at him, and the Puerto Rican guy kinda gave him a nod of agreement, and that was it. He had a chair," Kumpf concluded.

The rest of the evening Kumpf spent on the phone at the end of the max unit arranging to use one of his credit cards for bail, which he posted at 2 A.M. on his way out of the prison.

Kumpf remembered the max cell block that Tulloch was placed in as "real dark."

"It's like the first unit you go through on the way to the big cell blocks. It's real close to where the entrance and the guard station is, because that's where most of the shit flies and your most dangerous criminals go. The people who are most liable to hurt somebody or get hurt themselves go there," Kumpf said.

"There's four or five cells, and there's a bench and a phone that's at the end where you go into the cell block. The phone is right by where they open up and let you in, and they slide stuff to you, through a slot in the door that opens up that they put trays in. Those individual cells have got just wooden beds with the real thin plastic mattresses, you don't got pillows or nothing like that. Each one of these cells had like a stainless steel toilet/sink thing that was real small. No toilet seat or nothing. It looked like a water fountain on top of a toilet, and it didn't run like a sink, it ran like a water fountain.

"I wasn't there very long, but it didn't appear to me that, like, they had any real amenities. They were carrying around their own plastic Gatorade bottles, but they only had water in them, and that was it, man," Kumpf said.

"There was like a huge door that went into the next cell block which we couldn't see. When the guards came by us a few times to go into the huge cell block, you could hear a lot of noise in there. In between that area where the guards walked was a small table that had a TV on it, and if you wanted the TV channel changed when the guard walked by, you had to ask them to do it."

Kumpf felt that even in the unit segregated away from the main body of the prison population, Tulloch was at the bottom of the pecking order.

"I've been around in prison systems for a long time, and he had that look of someone who's become empty from either sexual abuse or beatings. He looked like he was already gone. He had that dead stare," Kumpf said. "You've heard of people in Vietnam developing that thousand-yard stare, and you kind of develop that in prison after a while. It's from trauma, man, that's where it comes from.

"I didn't even know it was him at first, until the guard told me. I said, 'That's the guy? That's him?' because he seemed so timid," Kumpf said.

While Tulloch languished among the heavy-duty felons in Haverhill, with one hour a day outside his cell, his friend Jimmy Parker was in his own brightly lit, comfortable room at the recently renovated Youth Detention Services Unit at the Tobey Building in a complex of state offices in Concord. When he arrived, there was something of a celebrity buzz about Jimmy, since the other kids had seen him on television, but that quickly wore off. The others had their own problems to worry about, and most of them only

stayed two or three weeks until their cases were resolved
with the courts before they moved on.

Instead of getting a cold meal slid through a slot in his
door twice a day, Parker was up each morning at 6 A.M.
for wake-up, and tidying up his room before reporting to
the cafeteria with the other juveniles in pre-trial detention.
After breakfast and a round of conversation, it was off to
school in another part of the building.

In the afternoons, residents on the "Third Floor" were
expected to work together on the day's homework, but once
it was done, there was plenty of free time before dinner to
watch TV, play board games, sort through the books, go to
the gym for basketball, or just hang out in the yard during
good weather. After sitting down to dinner, everyone had
to watch the 6 o'clock news afterwards (if anyone present
had actually *made* the 6 o'clock news, that segment would
be blocked out) and then it was reading or socializing until
lights-out at 9 P.M.

Workers on the Third Floor considered Parker a model
participant and reported that, aside from being a bit withdrawn, he seemed to be getting along fine with the staff
and the other teens at the facility.

Parker's family could visit him three times a week for
a few hours each time to sit with him and chat. By contrast,
Tulloch could have two family members visit him for one
hour sharp on Saturdays. The prisoner and his visitor have
to remain seated across from each other, and must have a
guard present the whole time.

Compared to Tulloch, Parker may as well have been on
vacation, but the day of reckoning was barreling at him,
and on May 24, he turned seventeen. By law, the Youth
Detention Services Unit had to transfer him to an adult
facility immediately. He was quietly put in a sheriff's
cruiser and driven north to Laconia and lodged in the maximum security unit of the Belknap County Department of
Corrections facility.

chapter 35

While Tulloch and Parker sat in jail cells miles apart, a nineteen-member Grafton County Grand Jury commenced its investigation into the charges to see whether formal indictments would be issued.

All four of the suspects' parents, Rob's younger brother Kienan Tulloch, and four of the boys' friends received notices in mid-March ordering them to appear in North Haverhill, New Hampshire, to testify as to what they knew of the boys' activities and whereabouts around the time of the killings.

The subpoenas were passed over to the Orange County Courthouse directly across the street from the Chelsea Public School on the South Common. Christiana Usenza was one of the four who were asked to testify.

Usenza had already been interviewed twice by detectives from both states. The first interview was the day after the boys had fled Chelsea, when Vermont State Police detectives and FBI agents sat down with her at Bob Sherman's home in Washington, Vermont, where she had lived on and off over the years.

The second interview was three days later, after the teens were captured in Indiana. Hanover and New Hampshire State Police detectives met with Christiana at Sherman's office in Montpelier.

Both interviews were about an hour long. "It was hard to talk so factually about something that's very, very emotional," Christiana later recalled.

Christiana told the authorities that she knew absolutely nothing about the murders, didn't know and had never even heard anything about the Zantops prior to their deaths, couldn't think of any link between Rob or Jimmy and the Zantops, had never seen any indication that Rob and Jimmy were interested in paramilitary activities or hate groups of any kind, and furthermore, didn't think either were capable of the homicides.

Christiana said that she had never been to Hanover with either of the pair. "They went every once in a while to go to movies. They went once to go rock climbing at a club there, but mostly, if they were going to go to movies, it would be in Montpelier or Burlington. It would have been rare," Christiana said.

She told the detectives that her mother Pamela Golds-borough was an artist and worked in a gallery, that neither she nor her mother had ever been a housecleaner, and that neither of them had ever been to the Zantops' residence in Etna.

"It is unbearable to hear their names mixed up in this mess," Christiana wrote in a statement to the press that was released while Tulloch and Parker were still on the run. "Whatever they are running from, it is not nearly as terrible as murder. I'm sure they are scared and just want to come home."

Christiana had an iron-clad alibi for the day of the kill-ings. She had spent the morning and mid-afternoon of January 27 taking the SAT tests for her college applications, and had then gone to work at the grocery store in Mont-pelier until 8:30 P.M. Many people had seen her both places.

As part of the process of arranging for Christiana to come to New Hampshire and testify before the grand jury, Kelly Ayotte sent her a letter saying that she was not a target of the ongoing investigation. Eventually, the attorney general's office stated to the press that Tulloch and Parker were believed to be the only individuals involved in the crimes.

Christiana and her mother had long-standing plans to take a vacation together in Mexico, and the New Hampshire

Grand Jury agreed not to subpoena her so that she could go on the two-week trip. In exchange for that consideration, Christiana agreed to appear voluntarily before the grand jury on April 20 and answer their questions.

Two other friends of Tulloch and Parker, 15-year-old Gaelen McKee and 17-year-old Zach Courts, received subpoenas from the grand jury to testify, as did Zach's father Tim Courts, although it was not clear why he was included.

New Hampshire authorities were also set to subpoena Michael, Diane, and Kienan Tulloch, along with John and Joan Parker, to find out what they knew of the events surrounding the weekend of January 27. Attorneys for both families wanted to avoid having parents and siblings forced to take the stand against the boys, so deals were worked out whereby all five family members were interviewed under oath by New Hampshire investigators. In exchange, the grand jury subpoenas were withdrawn. The Tullochs met for two hours with detectives at the Hanover Police Station. The Parkers were interviewed by investigators at their lawyer's office in White River Junction.

On March 19, at the Grafton County Courthouse, Zach Courts and Gaelen McKee spent the day being questioned by the grand jury. Tim Courts, who was under subpoena like the teens, did not end up testifying. Afterwards Tim Courts told reporters that the nineteen grand jurors had asked his son extensively about any knives that Rob and Jimmy possessed. They also asked whether or not either teen had ever mentioned the Zantops to Zach. Zach said they hadn't.

A month later, it was Christiana Usenza's turn before the grand jury, and shortly thereafter, she held her press conference at Kimbell Sherman Ellis' offices in downtown Montpelier.

"Good morning. I'm here to talk about my friends Robert and Jimmy. I don't know anything about this crime or any possible links or motives," Christiana began.

Asked if she thought either boy could have been capable

of the crime that occurred at the Zantops', Christiana was emphatic. "Not at all."

She said that in the six years she had known the pair, there had never even been a discussion of this kind of violence. "These are good people. I just can't imagine it. Robert was very, very smart," Christiana said, continuing that he was "Very witty, humorous, charming, on top of it. He knows what he wants."

Christiana said that neither boy struck her as even capable of violence. "They are very even-keeled, humorous people," she said.

Taken as a pair, Christiana didn't think Rob and Jimmy were any different together than when they were out and about as individuals. "I think it was probably about a year and a half ago when they started to be best friends, but they didn't spend every minute together. At one point Jimmy went to a different school, and Robert has other very close friends. They do their own stuff, like Jimmy takes music lessons," she said. "They thought of each other as very equal. They really respected each other's humor and thoughts, and they were very innovative and creative, and always doing things. They were very athletic."

Pressed about the weight of the evidence that seemed to be bearing down on the boys, Christiana said she still was hoping that police were wrong in charging them with the murders. "I'm not going to make any judgment right now until the trial is over. I hope that the trial produces the truth that they are innocent. I'm going to support them," she said. "I'm hoping with all my life that they have the wrong suspects.

"This is the most tragic thing I can imagine happening to a family and a community," Christiana said. "It's incredibly sad that they are in jail right now, and that this is at all connected with them in any way." She added that she also felt sorry for the Zantop family. "It must be really, really hard for the family to have no idea why this happened, and it was pretty brutal."

Christiana's lawyers, including her uncle, Richard Goldsborough, who was helping her through the process, advised her not to visit or contact either Rob or Jimmy pending her eventual appearance as a witness in the case.

"I hate having to think about this constantly," Christiana told the reporters. "It's always on my mind. It's like living a horror movie and picturing these murders."

Thinking about her friends and the case every day had taken a toll on Christiana's emotions, giving her nightmares in the process. "This is a very emotional, shattering thing," she noted. "Sometimes I want to wake up and just call Robert and go, 'Let's go rock climbing,' or 'Let's go play ultimate Frisbee,' and then I think, 'Oh, he's in jail,' and it's very hard."

On May 1, 2001, Rob Tulloch was taken out of the Grafton County Correctional Center and driven the extremely short distance to the Grafton County Courthouse next door for his formal arraignment.

Still wearing the same bird's-eye–patterned black-and-brown V-neck sweater that he had worn on the FBI jet from Indiana to New Hampshire back in February, Tulloch made a brief appearance before Judge Peter Smith to answer the grand jury's first-degree murder indictments.

Tulloch said one word during the three minute hearing. "Innocent."

His trial was scheduled for the spring of 2002.

chapter 36

Once Jimmy Parker was captured in Indiana and flown back to New Hampshire, the petition that the attorney general had signed asking courts to allow the dissemination of his name, picture, and other information about his case "for purposes of apprehension" became moot.

Moments after he touched down at the Lebanon Airport, Parker was whisked away into a legal black hole from which he was not expected to emerge until sometime in the year 2002.

As a juvenile Parker's records are not public. Even the status of the case to try to convert him from a juvenile to an adult for purposes of the upcoming trials is a topic which the legal system cannot comment on.

In theory, Parker could go right through the trial phase as a juvenile, and even if he were to be convicted of the double murders, given the maximum sentence, and released from prison on his twenty-first birthday, little, if anything, would be ever be known about his involvement in the case.

In theory.

In the last 15 years, ever since 1996, when the New Hampshire State Legislature dropped the age limit when offenders are considered adults down to seventeen, there hasn't been a juvenile charged with first-degree murder in New Hampshire who hasn't been certified as an adult by the time their trial rolled around.

In January 2001, the same month the Zantops were killed, the New Hampshire Supreme Court upheld a lower court ruling that a 16-year-old who shot and killed a 14-year-old should be tried as an adult.

Each case of adult certification is supposed to be weighed by the courts on its own merits, but the criteria seem to bode poorly for Parker's chances, given that he was just shy of his seventeenth birthday when he allegedly killed the Zantops. The judge considering the petition is supposed to take into account whether the alleged crime is of a serious nature—and it's hard to imagine a more serious case than this one—and other factors, including whether people were hurt, the strength of the state's evidence, and the sophistication and maturity of the minor. Finally the judge has to look at whether or not there is a reasonable likelihood that the accused minor can be rehabilitated by age 21 through the juvenile justice system.

Given those odds, the gravity of the crime, and the seeming weight of the state's circumstantial case against the teens, many legal observers were predicting Parker's best chance of avoiding a life sentence would be to "split, squeal, and cut a deal" against Tulloch, and exchange a full confession—assuming that he had one to give—for some form of leniency.

chapter 37

Whatever the ultimate outcome of the legal process now facing Robert Tulloch and Jimmy Parker, the events of January 27, 2001, and the weeks that followed have ripped deeply into the fabric of two communities separated by 23 miles, a scenic river, and a chasm of bewilderment and grief.

Residents in Etna who never bothered to lock their homes have suddenly begun making it a point to do so without fail. Dartmouth College reconsidered its long-cherished policy of leaving all of its buildings, dorms, and residence halls unlocked, and began issuing magnetic cards that were necessary to navigate the newly installed "perimeter control systems" throughout the campus. Chelsea faced a round of recriminations within their tiny school system and town government as parents and residents on both sides of the ideological divide tried to figure out who, if anyone, was to blame, and what, if anything, needs to be changed about the way the town's youth are being raised and educated.

Relations between Vermont law enforcement officials and their counterparts across the river in New Hampshire have been strained by the cultural differences between a law enforcement system used to sharing information with the public, and a system used to withholding it from the public. The out-of-state news media left New Hampshire irritated by what they saw as a largely adversarial relationship with officials who had viewed the press as the enemy when reporters tried to cover a case of profound interest to both the local communities and Dartmouth's far-flung family around the world. New Hampshire officials were furious at reporters whom they thought had filled the void of official information with what was viewed as little more than lurid fear-mongering and rank speculation.

But in the end, all of the antagonism and frustration that had boiled over around the edges of the case would still come down to one haunting question:

Why?

Why had the Zantops been murdered?

The lack of an official explanation for a motive prompted every conceivable sort of theory to be floated around the dinner tables and coffee shops of the Upper Valley. If some in the news media were willing to push into the voids that officials left open, the public was busy filling in any remaining blanks on their own.

Ultimately the question of why the Zantops were murdered will have to await the upcoming trials. Prosecutors with the New Hampshire Attorney General's Office have already pointed out that the law doesn't require them to establish a motive in order to prove the elements of first-degree murder—just that the defendants were there and that they did the killing, something that can be shown with physical evidence such as fingerprints and blood. Still, experienced trial observers have always felt that juries who hold defendants' lives in their hands want to know why one person would have wanted to kill another, and if that can't be explained, they are more likely to view that gap in the story as a reasonable doubt. Despite the pre-trial information blackout, the indications coming out of the New Hampshire Attorney General's Office as fall 2001 arrived were that prosecutors were gaining a better understanding of what they thought had prompted the double homicide.

Whoever is eventually held responsible for the Zantops' cruel deaths, and whatever eventually emerges as the reason for the stabbings, it's never going to be a good reason. Two law-abiding citizens who were also parents, friends, and respected teachers and colleagues should have been perfectly safe when they answered their doorbell on a quiet Saturday afternoon. The fact that they weren't is why the people of New Hampshire paid for one of the most intense and expensive investigations in the state's history, and why news organizations across the country devoted millions of dollars' worth of assets to covering the case and the Hanover Homicide Task Force's progress.

For all the sudden interest in shark attacks that swept the popular imagination again in the summer of 2001, it remains the predators amongst our own species who constitute the greatest threat to the rest of us. It's that sad, stark reality that, over the centuries, has prompted us to develop the elaborate police, investigative, and legal system we have today. It's sometimes hard for those involved in a case like the Zantop tragedy to remember, but there's no such thing as privacy when someone is murdered. All bets are off when the unyielding spotlight brought by the police and the press is shined under rocks and into darkened corners. That said, it's important to remember that if something terrible hadn't happened in the first place, none of what followed would have happened either.

The best the police can do is determine from the available evidence what actually happened. The best the legal system can do is to fairly and impartially consider that evidence, and place blame and exact justice for the horrible injustice done to the Zantops and those who loved them. The best the press can do is try to explain what happened to the larger interested public, because it is their absolute right to know the truth about anything so serious, regardless of how unpleasant or painful that might be. Because in the end, it is the American public that shoulders the responsibility for making society better and safer, and for preventing future tragedies from occurring.

When the lingering questions are finally answered, when the legalities are resolved, when the fate of the two teenagers in custody is finally decided, both Chelsea and Hanover will have to pick up the pieces and carry on.

Former Orange County Sheriff Sam Frank had just retired and moved from Chelsea to Virginia five months before the Zantop murders took place. He would watch the case unfold through the media and frequent calls from friends and relatives back home.

Frank said that even a clear, convincing answer to what happened that January weekend, and in the months preceding, would not be enough in the short run, but over time, he predicted, life would return to normal across East Hill, West Hill, and the village of Chelsea.

"I don't have a theory. I just think that it's sad that it happened. It's sad when anybody takes someone else's life," Frank said. "I don't like to see kids involved in trouble like this, or any kind of trouble. Of course, this whole thing is alleged, and we have to keep that in mind until it's done and over, but in the meantime, it sure has torn the town apart.

"Chelsea is a village where people all know each other. It's a small village," Frank noted. "Most of them up there are related and it's not that much different than any other small village in Vermont where they all bicker back and forth a little bit, but when the chips are down, they all pull together too . . . when you see a neighbor helping a neighbor at a fire, or when we've had flooding in the past and people came out and helped. Then you get the other ones that are in any community that are just not so good people and that's job security for the police. There are some bad people, but basically it's a good town and there are good people there, and this thing has kinda, because of the media, screwed things up a little bit and put one out against the other, but they'll work it out, and they'll get through it, particularly after the court has done its work. I think it's going to be a time before they heal, but they will," Frank said, adding, "They are a strong bunch."

Echoing much the same sentiment as Sheriff Frank, Dartmouth College President James Wright spoke in June to the graduating Class of 2001 at Dartmouth College's commencement. That morning, as the college was getting set for the day-long ceremony, hundreds of ribbons made up in the lilac color that had been Susanne's favorite were handed out. Printed in white letters on each ribbon were the words "Half & Susanne." By the time Wright rose to speak, the purple ribbons were displayed prominently on the elaborate and colorful robes of the Dartmouth faculty and the black-and-green gowns of the 1,571 graduating seniors.

As thousands of parents, students, and alumni looked on under a bright blue New Hampshire sky, Wright paused amidst the uplift and exhortations about the graduates' and the college's and the world's bright future, looked across the Hanover Green, and reflected on the murders that had consumed so much in the preceding five months.

"We know all too well that no community is apart from the intrusion of tragedy. No peaceable kingdom is immune from violence," Wright began. "But the test of a community is not whether it is protected from bad and evil, but rather how it responds to these things when they come upon us without warning or reason. By this test we can, in the midst of our pain, take pride. This community has responded well whenever challenged. The worst among us can never prevail so long as the best among us do not allow this to happen."

epilogue

After months of silence, events in the Zantop case began unfolding with great speed as the year ended and the legal strategies propelling the two accused teens toward trial took distinct turns away from each other.

Robert Tulloch and Jimmy Parker had begun 2001 as best friends, but by the time the year was over each was the other's worst enemy when it came to any hope of ever regaining their freedom in the wake of the events of January 27.

Robert Tulloch's public defenders announced on Friday, November 30 that Rob would be using an insanity defense to explain his actions when he got to trial, admitting to stabbing Half and Susanne to death, but arguing against legal culpability because of mental illness.

"In the course of representing Robert Tulloch and reviewing the facts of this case, the undersigned public defenders have become increasingly concerned that Robert suffers from a serious mental illness. The indications of mental illness were difficult to recognize because of Robert's intelligence and his particular personality; nevertheless, as the concerns grew, the undersigned public defenders sought an extensive evaluation of Robert by a highly qualified psychiatrist. That psychiatrist has now indicated that Robert does suffer from a severe mental defect or disease and that his acts were the direct result of the mental defect or disease. In light of this information, the defense must give notice that it will rely on the defense of insanity," attorneys Richard Guerriero and Barbara Keshen wrote in their notice to the court.

Legal observers quickly pointed out that with the seeming weight of the state's circumstantial case against Tulloch, the move smacked of desperation. No one has ever
successfully argued an insanity defense before a jury in
New Hampshire where the state didn't already stipulate to
the defendant's insanity prior to trial, newspapers noted.

The decision by Rob's team to defend him as involved
in the murders but insane left Jimmy Parker in a particularly
unattractive legal position. In October, behind closed doors,
Parker had been quietly certified as an adult for purposes
of his upcoming trial. Clearly the follower of the pair, there
was little Jimmy could now say in his own defense. He
could hardly claim that he didn't do it if Rob was busy
giving prosecutors and psychologists a detailed description
of the pair's role in the murders in order to better explain
the nuances of his own alleged insanity. At best, that left
Jimmy in the role of the sane henchman for a crazy person.

Whatever fate had in store for Rob, it was clear that
Jimmy was cooked. On December 7, 2001, a week after
Tulloch's attorneys made their announcement, Jimmy, now
17, was driven to the county complex in North Haverhill
to appear before Judge Peter W. Smith. Parker was there
to accept a plea bargain requiring him to admit to his role
in the killings, to give the state a complete account of what
had happened, and to eventually testify against Rob in open
court. It would also put Jimmy behind bars until he was at
least 41 years old.

It was an unusually warm, cloudless day for a New
Hampshire winter when Jimmy accepted the 25-year-to-life
deal. In a state filled with historic courtrooms, Jimmy stood
instead in the oddly modern egg-shaped chamber of the
Grafton County Superior Court with a single light from a
recessed dome over his head shining starkly down on him,
highlighting the pale prison complexion he had developed
in a summer away from the sun, the first of so many similar
summers to come.

With John Parker watching in ashen silence from the

front row only a few feet away, Jimmy Parker stood, look-ing pained, sporting the same short black haircut and dis-tinctive sideburns as his father. Jimmy acknowledged to Judge Smith that he understood the rights he was waiving by changing his plea and foregoing a trial. In blue prison pants and an untucked black polo shirt with the long sleeves bunched up over his elbows, Jimmy responded with a series of "I do"s and "Yes sir"s as Judge Smith ticked off the list of questions to determine whether he was competent to make such a decision. Judge Smith asked Jimmy if he was ill, or taking any prescription medications, or whether he was under the influence of any alcohol or other drugs. On the last question Jimmy perked up, mistaking Judge Smith's question about that morning's proceedings for a broader one. "Never," Jimmy said firmly. It was an unusual point of pride for somebody who was moments away from ad-mitting to having stabbed another human being to death for no apparent reason. Smith asked Jimmy if he knew the potential penalty had he faced trial on the original charges. "Life," Jimmy whispered back in reply.

A minute later, Court Clerk Bob Muh read out the new charge of accomplice to second degree murder in the death of just Susanne Zantop. Jimmy was asked how he pleaded. "Guilty," Jimmy said. It was an ending, but not an answer, for much of the state's case involving the death of the Zan-tops.

Even as Jimmy signed away more of his life than he had lived to date, the events in the courtroom were already moving past him. Parker's plea deal shifted the focus of the state's attention to the case it was still building against Robert Tulloch. A case in which officials admitted they still hadn't found the answer to the main question everyone had been asking . . . the simple question of "Why?"

In the following days, the Attorney General's Office would face a barrage of criticism from the Zantops' friends for having made any deal with Parker, but some would acknowledge privately that as frustrating as it was for them to see Parker cut even the slightest amount of slack, they too hoped the deal would eventually help answer the questions that still rolled around again and again when they tried to puzzle out what reason might lie behind the murders.

Kelly Ayotte read the court a brief, clinical rendition of the Zantop murders and the investigation that led to Parker and Tulloch's apprehension. The only new detail she let out to the sixty assembled reporters was that two extra chairs had been found in the Zantops' study when the investigators had combed through the wreckage of the crime scene, suggesting that perhaps Half had asked the boys to sit with him and discuss something before the melee started. It was a tantalizing clue, but still Ayotte insisted that the investigation had found no prior link between the boys and the Zantops that could explain their presence at the Etna house that Saturday afternoon. Whatever the state learned from Jimmy about the motive, whatever the details that Jimmy would be compelled to explain, it would all have to wait until Robert Tulloch's trial, scheduled for April 2002, before the public would see it revealed.